Baslow Church

THE OLD PARISH CHURCHES
OF DERBYSHIRE

Mike Salter

FOLLY PUBLICATIONS

ACKNOWLEDGEMENTS

The photographs and measured drawings in this book are mostly product of the author's fieldwork between 1973 and 1997. Old postcards, prints and brass rubbings are reproduced from originals in the author's collection. Thanks are due to Clare Sansom and Marjorie Salter who checked the text, and to Max Barfield and Beryl Brown for help with transport and accommodation during the mid 1990s.

ABOUT THIS BOOK

As with the other books about churches in this series (see the full list on the inside of the back cover) this book concentrates on the period before the Industrial Revolution of the late 18th century. Most furnishings and monuments after 1770 are not mentioned, but additions and alterations to the fabric usually are, although in less detail. Churches founded after 1770 are not mentioned in the gazetteer, nor do they appear on the map. They are, however, listed towards the back of the book.

The book is inevitably very much a catalogue of dates and names, etc. It is intended as a field guide and for reference rather than to be read from cover to cover. Occasionally there is a comment about the setting of a church but on the whole little is said about their position or atmosphere. The amount of material given for a particular church in this book is not necessarily a true indication of how interesting or attractive the building may be. Notable features of a church or the surrounding graveyard may lie outside the scope of this book. Visit them and judge for yourself. The gazetteer features Ordnance Survey grid references (these are the two letters and six digits which appear after each place-name and dedication) and the book is intended to be used in conjunction with the O.S. 1:50,000 scale maps.

Plans redrawn from originals in the author's field notes are reproduced to a common scale of 1:400. The buildings were measured in metres and only metric scales are given. A system of hatching common to all the plans is used to denote the different periods of work. The plans should be treated with care and cross-referenced with the text since there are some things difficult to convey on small scale drawings (e.g. stones of one period being reset or reused in a later period). In some cases walling is shown as of a specific century but is in fact difficult to date.

ABOUT THE AUTHOR

Mike Salter is 44 and has been a professional writer since he went on the Government Enterprise Allowance Scheme for unemployed people in 1988. He is particularly interested in the planning and layout of medieval buildings and has a huge collection of plans of churches and castles he has measured during tours (mostly by bicycle and motorcycle) of England, Ireland, Scotland and Wales since 1968. Wolverhampton born and bred, Mike now lives in an old cottage beside the Malvern Hills. His other interests include walking, model railways, board games, morris dancing, folk music, and he plays a variety of percussion instruments.

ISBN 1 87173133 X

Copyright 1998 by Mike Salter.
First published April 1998.
Folly Publications, Folly Cottage, 151 West Malvern Rd, Malvern, Worcs, WR14 4AY
Printed by Aspect Design, 89 Newtown Road, Malvern, Worcs, WR14 2PD

Chelmorton Church

CONTENTS

Introduction   Page   4

Gazetteer of Churches   Page   15

List of Later Churches   Page 102

Further Reading   Page 103

A Glossary of Terms   Page 104

Inside the front cover is a map of churches in the gazetteer.

Former chapel at Alderwasley, now a parish hall.

INTRODUCTION

Christianity was established in what was then the kingdom of South Mercia in 653 when the then king, Peada, married a daughter of Oswy, King of Northumberland, and as part of the marriage agreement brought back four missionaries. One of these, Diuma, was consecrated first bishop of the Mercians. At Repton, which was Peada's capital, Diuma established a double monastery for men and women. The church there was cruciform with four narrow arms extending from a wide central space possibly continued upwards as a central tower, whilst underneath was a crypt in which several kings were buried. This crypt, probably 9th century, still survives, being the only one of its type in Britain, although there are parallels in France and Germany. Most of the eastern half of the structure above, perhaps 9th century, but maybe later, has also survived later expansion and rebuilding. Foundations of a another cruciform Saxon church were found by excavations on the site of St Alkmund's prior to the building of a new road at Derby. A 9th century sarcophagus then found was taken to the museum. A panel with remarkable carved scenes from a coffin of c800 lies at Wirksworth. The churches of Aston-on-Trent, Bradbourne, and Stanton-by-Bridge all have a modest amount of Saxon masonry remaining in their naves with corners of the familiar so-called long and short work with long stones placed alternately upright and horizontal. Fragments of Saxon crosses usually with interlacing on the shaft and sometimes figures as well remain at over a dozen churches in Derbyshire, those at Bakewell and Eyam being the most remarkable.

About a third of the 170 churches described in the gazetteer have relics of the Norman period, nominally from 1066 until c1200, although it is doubtful if much or any of the remains predate the 1120s. In many cases just a font or doorway has survived later rebuilding but in several cases enough of the Norman building survives to judge its extent and character. The Saxon period had left a small number of mother churches, and during the 12th century stone chapels of more modest size were gradually provided in outlying villages and hamlets. Many of these chapels-of-ease later grew to be substantial churches in their own right, but some did not obtain full independence from the mother churches until the 19th century.

Saxon slab at Wirksworth

Ballidon, Barlow, and Caldwell are typical modest 12th century churches originally comprising a nave and chancel with a plain round arch between them. Chancels of this period were commonly square or nearly so in plan, just large enough to contain an altar and attendant priest and dimly lit by a small round headed window in each outer wall, the embrasures being widely splayed on the inside. Some chancels were a little longer and from 1200 onwards might have a narrow private doorway for the priest. The nave in which the congregation stood (seating was only provided at a much later date) was also dimly lighted by a few narrow windows. Normally there would be a doorway in the south wall, and sometimes one in the north wall opposite, and on the west gable would be a simple bellcote. Steetly Chapel represents a development on this layout in that it has an apsidal sanctuary beyond the square chancel, making a three celled plan. Steetly is lavishly decorated, with rich carvings around the doorway and arches, and small columns called nook-shafts flanking its windows. Indeed it is one of the grandest of the smaller Norman churches in Britain.

Saxon crypt at Repton

Nine churches in Derbyshire have a tower of the period 1130-1200 at the west end of the nave instead of just a bellcote. These churches are Aston-on-Trent, Brampton, Bradbourne, Brassington, Muggington, Ockbrook, Thorpe, Tissington, and Whitwell. Most of them have been heightened or altered later with inserted windows and added buttresses and battlements. Melbourne has a well preserved and little altered Norman church on an altogether more ambitious plan. It is cruciform with a central tower and transepts between the chancel and the nave, which has side aisles and a splendid west front with two towers. This produces a plan form common enough in cathedral and abbey churches but unique amongst Norman churches of purely parochial status. Originally the chancel ended in an apse and there was an apsidal chapel opening off the east side of each transept. No other apses are known in Derbyshire but some probably existed prior to later rebuilding. Bakewell has some remains of another large Norman church with an aisled nave but there the intended pair of west towers seem to have never been completed and the arches into them have been walled up by the late 12th century when the present west front was built. Several other churches had at least one aisle by the year 1200, usually as the result of a later addition to give more space for a growing congregation than as part of an original plan. In each case the piers are round in section until keeling appears c1200. Early 12th century arcades have plain round arches. The next development is to make the arches stepped, then one or both steps may have slight chamfering. By the 13th century, when the arches are usually pointed rather than round, both steps would normally have a considerable chamfer.

Sandiacre has a particularly fine Norman south doorway. Doorways of this period commonly have a semi-circular panel called a tympanum set under the round arch, and there are examples with interesting carvings in several churches, notably Ault Hucknall, Hognaston and Parwich. Whitwell also has a Norman clerestory, a rarity in a parish church, but Melbourne also has one. For Norman fonts, see page 11.

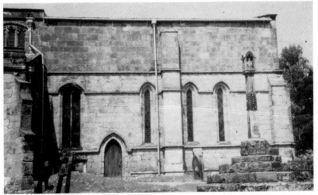

13th Century chancel at Doveridge

Blocked doorway at Ault Hucknall

The chancel of Southwell Minster begun in 1234 perhaps inspired the design of the nearly contemporary chancel at Ashbourne. It was dedicated in 1241, as commemorated on a contemporary brass plaque, a very rare survival. Later in the century Ashbourne was given a central tower with transepts. Chesterfield and Wirksworth have the same layout, on a similarly generous scale. These churches all had the unusual feature of eastern aisles to the transepts, a feature also found in a south transept (now rebuilt) at Bakewell, where there is another central tower, and probably inspired by the transept east aisles of c1225-50 at Lichfield Cathedral. In each of these churches the upper parts of the towers were not built until the early 14th century. Kedleston is also cruciform with a central tower, whilst Monyash is cruciform with a west tower. Darley Dale and Hartington are similar but there the towers are later. Doveridge has a fine chancel of this period and also a west tower converted from an older one, whilst of nearly twenty other west towers of the 13th century surviving in Derbyshire the best are Breadsall and Eckington. Aisles of the 13th century are common, some churches having two of them, although often of slightly different periods. Indeed most of the medieval churches in Derbyshire have or had at least one medieval aisle, and about half had an aisle on each side of the nave. The pointed arch was now in vogue and there is a variety of pier forms, with quatrefoils shaped piers as well as circular and octagonal ones.

The fine chancel at Norbury begun c1300 introduces us to the 14th century and the Decorated style of architecture. Other fine chancels are Sandiacre of the 1340s, Chaddesden of the 1350s, and Taddington of the 1370s. There is another of the 1360s at Tideswell, where the whole of the spacious cruciform church is datable to c1320-1400. Much of Chesterfield church was rebuilt in this period and it has the unusual feature of a transept chapel with a polygonal apse. A rare feature of a number of chancels in Derbyshire of this period is a stone book-rest built into the north wall, as at Chaddesden, Crich, Etwall, Mickleover, Spondon, and Taddington.

At least twenty towers are 14th century work. Early towers are normally either unbuttressed or have thin pilasters, but from about 1280 diagonal buttresses of bolder projection were used, although many 14th and 15th century towers have pairs of buttresses at right angles at each of the two western corners. Spires are numerous but are hard to date accurately and in any case have usually required 18th or 19th century rebuilding. Plain broach spires start in the mid to late 13th century and continue into the 14th century, examples being Baslow, Brampton, Breaston, Hope, Ockbrook, Rosliston and Taddington. In Derbyshire 14th and 15th century spires are often of a narrower type recessed behind an embattled or pierced parapet.

Mickleover

Church Broughton

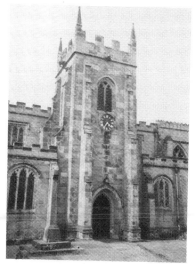

Norbury

Crich

Denby

Tideswell

Derbyshire Church Towers

Chaddesden Church

The Perpendicular style, so called because of a tendency to exaggerate verticals, first appears in Derbyshire with the tower of the 1380s at Tideswell and the east window of the 1390s at Ashbourne. The style then remained in vogue until the reformation of the English church by Henry VIII in the 1530s and 40s. Derbyshire has surprisingly little of this period compared with other English counties. Many churches have an aisle or arcade of this period, or a clerestory often with battlements above, inserted windows are common, and there are nearly thirty towers, but churches which are completely or mostly 15th or early 16th century are rare, the modest building at Shirland being the only example. The tower at All Saints, Derby is the largest and most ornate of its type, having tall bell-openings of a type rare in Derbyshire. A small group of towers are adorned with eight pinnacles as at Barlborough, Elvaston, and Youlgreave. In the eastern part of Derbyshire are a group of churches with 15th century porches with unusual pointed tunnel-vaults. The 16th century porch at Denby is also vaulted, and there is a 14th century porch with a rib-vault at Tideswell. From the 14th century onwards trade-guilds and lords began to found chantry chapels in churches. Sometimes these were accommodated in already existing aisles and transepts but at Hathersage and Norbury and elsewhere 15th century chapels were added for this purpose or to provide a family burial place.

Derbyshire is no exception to the general rule of there being little of architectural interest dating from the Elizabethan period in parish churches, despite the many monuments and some furnishings. The chapel begun in 1593 at Risley is only of minor interest. Also quite humble are a chapel of 1625 at Buxton, and the slightly later churches of Carsington, Heage and Turnditch. Although as late as 1662 the church at Foremark is still quite gothic but with a symmetry of elevation not normal in medieval buildings. It is additionally dignified with a west tower. The Frechville chapel at Staveley is the only other work of note from the 17th century.

East end of Dronfield Church

Elmton Church

Trusley of 1713 is the first complete Derbyshire church in the classical style but in importance it is totally overshadowed by the work of 1723-5 at All Saints, Derby, designed by James Gibbs and on a par with his work in London. The chapel at Barton Blount is mostly of 1714, Halter Devil Chapel is of 1723, Pinxton is of 1750, Holbrook has work of 1761 and Elmton is of 1773, but the only other notable building is the octagonal nave with an ambulatory at Stoney Middleton, built in 1759.

Between 1830 and 1914 most of the medieval parish churches in England were restored and refurnished. Some needed extensively rebuilding because they had been allowed to decay, or were no longer large enough to accommodate a growing congregation, but others were renovated just because it was fashionable to do so. A lucky few escaped with just minor repairs and perhaps the inconspicuous addition of a vestry or porch, but many churches lost interesting architectural features, monuments and furnishings. Effigies, glass, screens and other interesting furnishings were commonly moved from their original positions. The items described in the gazetteer are just a fraction of the treasures that once existed in these churches.

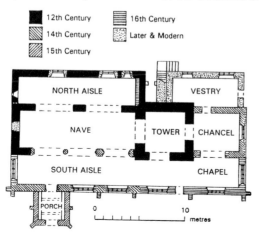

- 12th Century
- 14th Century
- 15th Century
- 16th Century
- Later & Modern

Plan of Ault Hucknall Church

Barlow Church

Font at Somersal Herbert

Font at Ashbourne

Pulpit at Chesterfield

Doorways and masonry styles can help to date the different parts of old churches but usually the shape and style of the windows is the best evidence. However it should be remembered that the windows may be later insertions in an older wall or earlier openings reused. During the 12th century windows gradually increased in size from the tiny round-headed openings of the Saxon and Norman periods to the long lancets with pointed heads in the chancels of the 1230s and 40s at Ashbourne and Doveridge. Windows of two lights appear in the belfry stages of the Norman towers at Brassington and Thorpe but early windows are otherwise of just one opening, made large if necessary. By the late 13th century a common form in Derbyshire was a pair of lancets with the spandrel between their heads pierced. From these were developed windows of three or more lights with intersecting tracery at the turn of the 13th and 14th centuries. The Norbury chancel of c1300-5 illustrates the next stage in which foils and trefoils are placed between the intersections. With this we have reached the Decorated style. The north transept at Ashbourne illustrates another variant of this period in which a quatrefoil breaks the pattern of intersections at the top. Beside it is an example of reticulated or net-like tracery with tiers of small arches one upon another, and typical of the middle two quarters of the 14th century. Flowing tracery with flower-like forms can be seen at Spondon, Tideswell and Taddington. Sandiacre and Chaddesden have star-like forms of tracery of a type common in Kent. Many 14th century windows in the county are straight-headed.

The Ashbourne east window of c1392-9 heralds the Perpendicular style with few if any breaks to the verticality of the mullions resulting in long panels. Other large windows in this style are rare in Derbyshire. Straight-headed windows become more common, especially in places where not much vertical space was available anyway, as in clerestories commonly added to naves at this time. Some of these windows have minimal tracery, just cusping in the four-centred heads of the lights. By the early 16th century even the cusping was sometimes dispensed with, and then it was but a short step to make the lights round headed instead of with flattened pointed arches. However gothic lasted long in Derbyshire churches and was still in occasional use after the Civil War. The classical style with large rounded headed windows comprised of a single light without tracery only appears in the 1720s at All Saints, Derby, and then became the norm for the rest of the century.

All the different medieval architectural styles reappeared during the 19th century restorations, Norman being favoured in the 1840s, early and middle Gothic later, and late Gothic at the turn of the 19th and 20th centuries.

Frechville Chapel, Staveley Church

Over twenty Norman fonts survive in the parish churches of Derbyshire, being in some instances the only relic of that period to survive later rebuilding of the fabric. The two most notable are of c1200, one of lead at Ashover, and one with interesting carvings (and the unique feature of an attached stoup) now lying at Youlgreave, but originally at Elton. Earlier fonts at Hognaston and Eyam have arcades and there are others with interlaced arches at Ockbrook, Kirk Hallam, and Somersal Herbert, whilst that at Tissington has incised animals. There are only a handful of fonts from each of the subsequent decades. Ashbourne has the best of the 13th century ones, and Bakewell the best of the few 14th century examples. Later medieval fonts often have shields, quatrefoils and other simple motifs on the sides, an octagon being the commonest form. A number of fairly plain 17th century fonts bear dates in the 1660s. In the 18th century fonts tend to be baluster shaped, as at Breaston, Litton, Kedleston, and Willington.

By the time of the Reformation of the 1530s the interiors of churches that had been bare and poorly lighted in the 12th and early 13th centuries had been transformed. Large new windows admitted more light, despite being filled with stained glass. Early stained glass figures remain at Ashbourne and Dalbury, and 14th century ones at Cubley, whilst Norbury has shields and grisaille glass of c1307. Later glass remains at Ault Hucknall, Caldwell, Egginton, and Morley has some fine work of the 1480s from Dale Abbey. Internal walls were usually whitewashed and then painted with biblical scenes or lives of saints. Wingerworth has 12th century wall paintings and there are others of c1300 and the 14th century at Dale Abbey and Melbourne. In the 15th century benches were provided for the congregation, surviving examples usually having poppy heads at the ends. The larger churches had miserichords or hinged seats with lips to support the behinds of choristers when standing. No complete sets now survive in Derbyshire, just the odd one or two seats at Bakewell and Tideswell. The growth of choirs is one reason why chancels became much larger and few of the early small ones survive. Chancels often had built into the south wall two or three seats called sedilia for the use of the clergy. Near the sedilia would be the piscina or basin used for rinsing and draining the mass vessels.

Old doors occasionally survive but more common is the reuse of medieval ironwork on a more recent door. Floor tiles also occasionally remain. Several churches have 17th or 18th century communion rails. Church plate was usually secured in a chest with iron bands. A common arrangement was for there to be three locks so that the vicar and two church wardens each had to be present with his own single key before the chest could be opened. Medieval pulpits are rare and indeed lengthy sermons only became the norm in the 16th century when English replaced Latin as the liturgical language and at last commoners could begin to understand what was being said in the services. Jacobean pulpits are common in other English counties but there are few in Derbyshire. The best are at Chesterfield and Dronfield. Kedleston should be noted as having a complete set of wooden furnishings of c1700.

In the later medieval period it was normal for chancels and chapels to be divided off by screens in the form of traceried timber partitions. The screen dividing off the chancel from the nave was often surmounted by a loft reached by a staircase in a sidewall. Towards the nave the loft would have a parapet upon which was mounted a rood or crucifix, hence the terms rood-loft and rood-screen. The loft was used by musicians (important in an age when few churches could afford an organ), and by the performers of religious plays which were a means of conveying Biblical ideas to a congregation containing many who could neither read nor write in any language nor understand spoken Latin. Wingerworth has the only medieval loft now remaining in Derbyshire, an unusual one without a screen below it. Of the early 14th century are the rare stone screen at Ilkeston and the timber one at Kirk Langley. Later medieval screens are at Ashover, Ashbourne, Bakewell, Chaddesden, Darley Dale, Elvaston and Chesterfield and Fenny Bentley where in each case the groining of the former loft also remains. There is a low stone screen at Chelmorton.

Interior of Wingerworth Church

Tomb in Norbury Church

Brass at Mugginton

Incised slab at Darley Dale

There are 22 engraved brasses, 22 incised alabaster slabs inlaid with pitch, and about stone or alabaster effigies earlier than 1540 in the parish churches of Derbyshire. The best of the English alabaster quarries was at Chellaston, near Derby, so it comes as no surprise to find a high proportion of local monuments being made of it. Many of the later effigies and slabs seem to have been made in workshops at Burton-on-Trent. The earliest monument of this material in the county is that with two canopied half figures at Bakewell. The finest of the tomb chests are those at Ashbourne, Norbury and Youlgreave. Earlier monuments of note are the female effigies of the 1220s or 30s at Brampton and Scarcliffe, and the sunk heads in quatrefoils in the floor at Kedleston. The earliest brass is that of 1399 at Dronfield. Hathersage has two of the 15th century, plus another of the 1560s. There are good collections of both pre-reformation and post-reformation monuments at Ashbourne, Bakewell, Chesterfield, and Norbury. Bakewell in particular has a large number of 12th and 13th century headstones and coffin lids with foliated crosses and vocational symbols.

Brass at Morley

Monument in Bakewell Church

In Derbyshire effigies of the period 1540-1650 are as common as those from the medieval period. Many of them continue the traditional medieval tomb chest type with recumbent effigies, an incised slab or brasses on top. However the majority of tombs of this period are placed against a wall with some sort of back panel or even a canopy. Monuments of c1560 at Etwall and Wirksworth illustrate the old and new types. Tombs of c1600-25 with canopies occur at Bakewell, Derby All Saints, Sudbury and Wilne. Of more modest monuments a common type is the sort where couples are depicted kneeling facing each other, as at Bakewell, Chesterfield, Tissington, and Youlgreave, and later brasses often show this sort of scene as well. Incised slabs continue along with brasses, but the quality of both tends to rapidly deteriorate after 1540. A brass of c1580 to a bishop at Tideswell is still in the medieval tradition. Effigies at Chesterfield and Fenny Bentley are depicted in burial shrouds, and so is the figure on a very late brass at Beeley.

The emphasis on effigies gradually decreased during the 17th century, Duffield, Edensor and Sutton-on-the-Hill having early 17th century tomb chests without effigies. Fully three dimensional monuments become rarer in the late 17th and 18th centuries when the most common type of monument is a tablet with a lengthy inscription with or without an architectural surround, urns, cherubs, or symbols of death, a profession, or claim to fame. Good collections of late monuments are at Brampton, Eckington, Kedleston, and many churches have single good examples.

ALDERWASLEY *St Margaret* SK 324534

The 16th century single chamber has a south doorway with square panels with crude designs on its lintel. The east window and one on the south have arched lights. Older work may survive in the north wall. A new church of 1850 lies by the hall.

ALFRETON *St Martin* SK 407559

The church lies by the entrance to the grounds of the hall at the west end of the town. The tower arch looks 13th century but tyhe rest of the diagonally buttressed west tower is 15th century. The nave arcades are of five bays, that on the south being of the 1320s, whilst that on the north dates from the 1868 restoration by T.C.Hine. It was then that the fifth bay on each side was created and the original east window was moved to the north aisle west end. The chancel was enlarged in 1899-1901 and is mostly of that period but projecting from it on the north side is a medieval vestry vaulted in stone with unmoulded transverse arches. The aisle windows with heads as label stops are mostly 15th century, and the south porch is also of that period and has an ogival-headed niche over the outer entrance. The brass figures are missing from a wall monument to John Ormonde and Joan Chaworth, d1507. There is also a very fine monument without an effigy to George Morewood, d1792, and a tablet to George Bonsall, d1797.

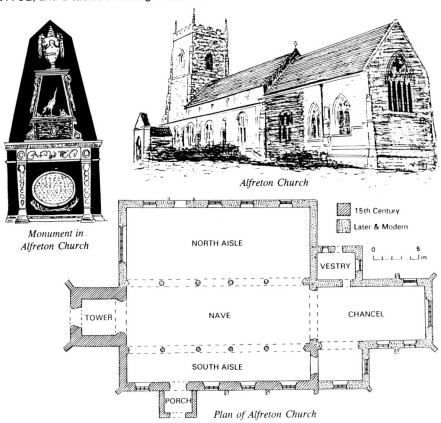

Alfreton Church

Monument in Alfreton Church

NORTH AISLE

▨ 15th Century

▩ Later & Modern

0   5
⌊⌊⌊⌊ ⌊⌊⌋ m

VESTRY

TOWER NAVE CHANCEL

SOUTH AISLE

PORCH

Plan of Alfreton Church

Allestree Church

Doorway at Alsop-en-le-Dale

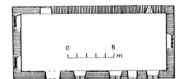

Plan of Alderwasley Church

ALLESTREE   *St Edmund*   SK 348398

The 13th century west tower has broad low buttresses. The fine Norman south doorway has chevrons and an order of colonettes with beakheads biting them and the same motif in the roll-moulding of the arch. The outer label has leaf patterns.
The rest was entirely rebuilt in 1865-6 by Stevens & Robinson of Derby.

ALSOP-EN-LE-DALE   *St Michael*   SK 160551

The Norman nave has an original south doorway with double chevrons on the voussoirs. The imposts of the chancel arch are also original. The imitation Norman west tower of 1882-3 was designed by F.J.Robinson. The tiny original Norman chancel has been replaced by a 19th century one the same width as the nave.

ALVASTON   *St Michael*   SK 393334

The church was entirely rebuilt in 1855-6 by H.I.Stevens but there survive a Saxon coffin lid with a large primitive cross and some ironwork probably by Bakewell of Derby from a reredos given to the church by Charles Benskin, d1739.

ASHBOURNE   *St Oswald*   SK 176465

This church is one of the largest and finest in Derbyshire and lies at the west end of the town. It is assumed that an important Saxon church once lay on this site and traces of a Norman crypt were discovered in 1913. The oldest part of the present church is the splendid chancel over 24m long, divided into five bays. The very rare brass inscription in the south transept with Lombardic script recording the dedication of the church in 1241 must refer to the completion of the chancel, which has pairs of lancets in each of the three eastern bays. The lancets have filleted nook shafts inside and there is a fine south doorway with six orders of renewed colonettes. The sedilia with filleted shafts have been reset at a higher level to correspond with a rise in the floor level. In the 1390s the original east lancets were replaced by a seven light window in the Perpendicular style and then or somewhat earlier the paired lancets in the fourth bay from the east were replaced by three light windows with reticulated tracery. In 1876-8 George Gilbert Scott restored the chancel and added the battlements. The western bays of the chancel have arches opening into the wide eastern aisles of the transepts. The transepts themselves have pairs of western lancets with original stained glass medallions of Nativity scenes in the northernmost one. The transepts and the crossing arches may be mid 13th century but the transept east aisles can hardly be earlier than c1290-1300. The north transept end wall has above an asymmetrically placed doorway a five light window with reticulated tracery likely to be of c1320-50. Somewhat earlier is the transept aisle north window of five lights with intersected tracery with a quatrefoil at the top, whilst the pairs of triple lancets in the aisle east wall look still earlier. The south transept also has an asymmetrically placed doorway, over which is a seven light window with intersected tracery, party with cusping, i.e. probably of c1300-20. A seven light window probably of the 1390s fills the entire south end wall of the transept aisle. The heavy buttresses must be of the same period. The part of this aisle now divided off to provide vestries is lighted by a four light 14th century east window. The low clerestory on the transepts and nave is of the 1520s.

Ashbourne Church

South Transept at Ashbourne

The western part of Ashbourne church is rather irregularly laid out, possibly as the result of the survival of the south wall of a narrower Saxon or Norman nave until the south aisle was built at the beginning of the 14th century. The nave is set on an axis further north than the chancel and its west end inclines to the north. Beside a big buttress giving extra support to the NW tower arch is a narrow arch leading from the nave into the north transept. There is no north aisle, although the generous width of the nave and the south aisle partly compensate for this. They are divided by a four bay arcade with leaf capitals and heads on the piers. The stepped lancets in the nave north wall may be of the last years of the 13th century. The east respond has a green man and heads likely to be of Edward I and his chief minister Walter Langton, Bishop of Lichfield. Heads on the next two capitals may be the future Edward II and his cousin Thomas, Earl of Lancaster, the smiling woman behind the latter probably being his mother Blanche d'Artois. The wide west doorway opening into the nave SW corner dates from the restoration of 1881-2 by G.L.Abbot. The west wall still bears scars resulting from an attack by Parliamentary troops in 1644. Until the 19th century there were north and south doorways into the nave and aisle, the latter having a two storey porch in front. Then also still visible were wall paintings of St Christopher, the Crucifixion, the Lord's Prayer, and the names and emblems of the twelve tribes of Israel. The aisle roof is late medieval, but much restored. At the west end of the aisle is a 13th century font with small fleur-de-lis between trefoil arches. The tower upper parts and spire reaching to 64m are early 14th century. The belfry has two-light windows on each side with transoms and is capped by a pierced trefoil parapet. The spire has four tiers of dormer windows. It was damaged by a gale in 1698 and required rebuilding twice in the 18th century and once in the 19th century.

The transept east aisles later became the chapels of the two leading families of the district. Little of interest remains in the south chapel, where the Bradbournes founded a chantry in 1483, but two 15th century stall ends, probably from Norbury, remain in the transept. The tombs with effigies of John Bradbourne, d1483, and his wife Anne Vernon, and Sir Humphrey Bradbourne, d1581, and his wife have been moved to the north chapel, which contains monuments to the Cockaynes. The oldest effigies are those of John and Edmund Cockayne, d1372 and 1403 respectively, set on a low tomb chest with quatrefoil panels, a fleuron frieze and battlements. Next are those of Sir John Cockayne, d1447, and his wife on a tomb chest with angels with shields separated by panel tracery. The incised slab depicting John Cockayne, d1504, and his wife is badly defaced. Better preserved is that on a tomb chest with foiled panels to Sir Thomas Cockayne, d1537, and his wife. Another tomb chest adorned with angels bears brasses depicting Francis Cockayne, d1538, and his wife under an architectural setting. The oldest of several monuments to the Boothbys, successors to the Cockaynes, is the urn to Ann, nee Cavendish, d1701. Much more famous is the white marble effigy by Thomas Banks of Penelope Boothby, d1793, aged nearly six, which is said to have reduced Queen Charlotte to tears when exhibited at the Royal Academy. Also in the north chapel are a medieval screen, a painted 15th century panel (probably from another screen), and some architectural fragments, including a Saxon stone with interlace and a Norman stone with chevrons. In an ogival arched recess in the chancel north wall is a monument to Robert de Kniveton, d1471. There are also effigies of Sir Thomas Cockayne, d1592, and his wife.

ASHFORD-IN-THE-WATER *Holy Trinity*   SK 185698

The features which survived the 1868 rebuilding are the 13th century west tower with 15th century battlements and pinnacles, the 14th century three bay north arcade, a Norman tympanum over the south doorway with a Tree of Life flanked by a lion and a pig, a 15th century font, a Jacobean pulpit, and Royal Arms of 1724.

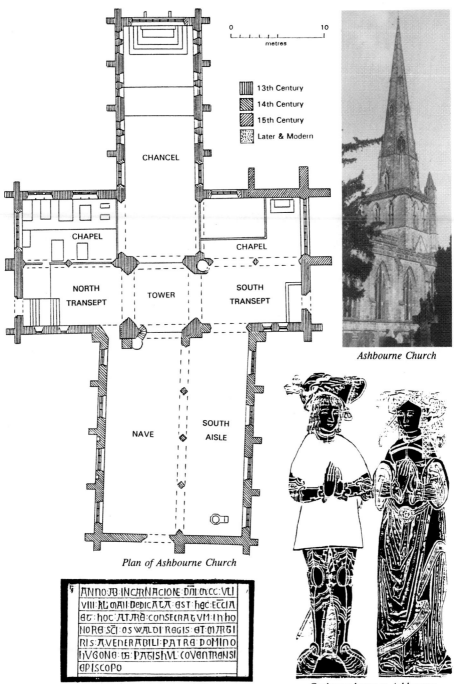

13th Century

14th Century

15th Century

Later & Modern

CHANCEL

CHAPEL

CHAPEL

NORTH TRANSEPT

TOWER

SOUTH TRANSEPT

NAVE

SOUTH AISLE

Plan of Ashbourne Church

Ashbourne Church

ANNO JB·INCARNACIONE·DĪI·ᴍ·cc·VLI
VIII·ᴋL·ᴍAII·DEDICATA·EST·hEC·ECCIA
ET·hoc·ATJRE·CONSECRATVM·IN·ho
NORE·SCI·OSWALDI·REGIS·ET·ᴍIJRTI
RIS·A·VENERABILI·PATRE·DOMINO
hVGONE·DE·PATISHVL·COVENTRANSI
EPISCOPO

Dedication Inscription at Ashbourne

Cockayne brass at Ashbourne

Ashover Church

ASHOVER   *All Saints*   SK 349631

The oldest and most interesting feature is the lead font of c1200 with many figures under arches. It is inferior in quality to most of the other thirty Norman lead fonts in England but is similar to that at Dorchester Abbey in Oxfordshire. The late 13th century south doorway is the oldest part of the building itself. The north aisle and the chancel with trefoiled-arched recesses in the north wall are 14th century. The aisle was given an extra fourth bay when a south aisle was added at the turn of the 15th and 16th centuries. The aisle has a large quint leading into the chancel. The straight-headed windows are all late-medieval. The diagonally buttressed west tower is 14th century but was not completed until after 1419, when the Babington family came to Ashover. It has straight headed belfry openings and a recessed spire rising 39m high. There is a very fine alabaster tomb chest with effigies of Thomas Babington, d1518, and his wife, who donated the rood screen. There are brasses depicting Rector Philip Eyre, d1504, and James Rolleston, d1507, and his wife with children kneeling below them. The plain panelled pulpit is late 17th century.

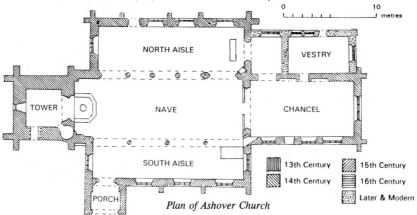

Plan of Ashover Church

ASTON-ON-TRENT   *All Saints*   SK 415294

The lower parts survive of the eastern corners of a nave probably of Late Saxon date. To it was added a Norman west tower which retains its original arch to the nave and a west doorway and windows with nook-shafts and arches with chevrons. The bold diagonal buttresses and the top stage are 15th century and the battlements with obelisk pinnacles are probably 17th century. The aisles are late 13th century and have arcades of three bays with short circular piers. The ogival arched north doorway and the south aisle windows with reticulated tracery are 14th century and the north windows and the embattled clerestory are 15th century. The 14th century chancel is embattled and has straight-headed south windows with a transom band of tracery. The plain octagonal font set on five shafts is 13th century. There are recumbent effigies of an early 15th century civilian and his wife holding hands on a tomb chest with angels holding shields.

AULT HUCKNALL   *St John the Baptist*   SK 468653

The church lies alone except for just one farm. It has a 15th century crossing tower perched on a west arch which looks Norman and a narrow east arch which may be still earlier. The nave and north aisle are certainly no later than the 1130s and are divided by a two bay arcade with a rectangular pier. The nave has a blocked narrow west doorway and the aisle west window has a tympanum carved with what may be St Margaret emerging from the body of the Devil and a lamb and cross, whilst on the lintel is a man (probably St George) in combat with a dragon. Of the 14th century are the nave roof with big tie-beams and coarse trefoil tracery above, the west window with reticulated tracery, and the south porch with a pointed tunnel vault with transverse arches. The furnishings mostly date from a restoration of 1885-8 by Butterfield but the south aisle east window has stained glass featuring the Crucifixion dated 1527, below which is a monument of 1627 in an Italianate style to Anne Keighley, wife of the first Earl of Devonshire. A slab in front of this monument commemorates the philosopher Thomas Hobbes, who died at Hardwick Hall in 1679.

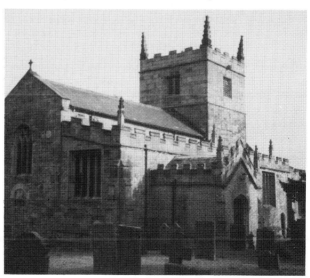

Aston-on-Trent Church   *Ault Hucknall Church*

Bakewell Church from the SE

Bakewell Church from the SW.

BAKEWELL   *All Saints*   SK 216685

The stem of an early 9th century cross in the churchyard with vine-scrolls, animals and defaced human figures shows that this was an important religious centre at an early date. Many fragments of the Saxon and Norman periods, including an 11th century cross-shaft with interlace patterns moved here from Two Dales, lie in the porch and the west end of the north aisle. Externally the west front is late 12th century work with a central doorway with two orders of nook-shafts. Earlier in the 12th century the nave was given aisles with unmoulded arches on rectangular block piers, the westernmost of which survive on each side. There also remain at the west ends of the aisles arches intended originally to open into a pair of west towers, so that the west front as then planned would have been 4.5m further beyond where the present west wall now stands. A double plinth with roll-mouldings is a relic of a former Norman apse. The present three-bay chancel is late 13th century and has windows with pairs of lancets with pierced spandrels above. Original are the priest's doorway and the triple sedilia and the piscina with a twin arch with pointed trefoil cusping. During the same period the north aisle was widened so that its outer wall was flush with the north transept, and new windows similar to those in the chancel were provided in both aisles. In 1825 the spire of the central tower was taken down, and the tower itself in 1830. A new tower and spire in a 14th century style and 5m lower than the originals were erected during a drastic rebuilding of the church by William Flockman in 1841-52. The work also included the complete rebuilding of the very large south transept with a three bay eastern aisle originally erected in the 1220s and 30s (but apparently given new east windows in the early 14th century), the provision of new arcades, the addition of a large vestry beyond the north transept, and the renewing of the aisle windows. Of the 15th century are the south porch, the nave clerestory and battlements, and the large three-light north window of the north transept with a transom and panel tracery at the top.

The chancel furnishings date from a restoration of that part in 1879-82 by G.G.Scott and Temple Moore, but three much repaired 14th century miserichords remain among the choir stalls. In the porch are some 13th century tiles and a fine collection of headstones and coffin lids with foliated crosses (some with vocational symbols) found during the 1840s restoration. The Vernon Chapel in the east aisle of the south transept has a 15th century screen and contains many monuments. The earliest and least well preserved is an effigy of Sir Thomas Wendesley, d1403. There is a modest alabaster tomb chest with small figures to John Vernon, d1477. The Royley family of carvers at Burton-on-Trent are thought to have made the effigies of Sir George Vernon, d1567, and his two wives. There are wall-monuments with kneeling figures of Sir John Manners, d1584 and his wife Dorothy Vernon, and Sir George Manners, d1623, and his wife. On the transept west wall is a small brass depicting Latham Woodroofe, d1648. By far the finest monument at Bakewell lies in the chancel and is of a type more common in the 16th and 17th centuries although actually as early as c1365-75. It has full frontal alabaster demi-figures of Godfrey Foljambe, d1377, and his second wife Avena Ireland set under a fine crocketed canopy with shields above.

BALLIDON   *All Saints*   SK 203544

The church lies in a field and is a 12th century building comprising nave and chancel with a plain unmoulded arch between them. The north doorway is blocked and the west window has been given a new head. The other windows were replaced in the 1882 restoration when a porch was added on the south side and an organ and vestry space on the north side.

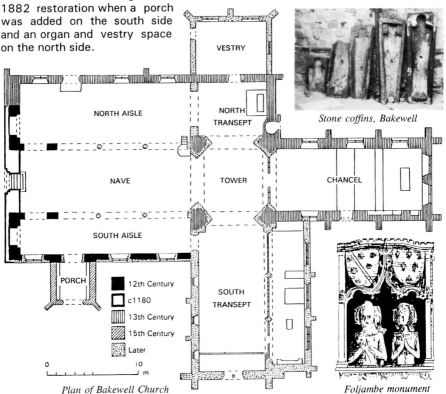

Stone coffins, Bakewell

Plan of Bakewell Church

Foljambe monument

BARLBOROUGH   *St James*   SK 477773

The church was once dedicated to St Mary. The north aisle was rebuilt in 1894-9, as were the south arcade and clerestory. The four bay north arcade is of the 1190s and has round arches with two slight chamfers and waterleaf capitals on the piers, one of which is a keeled quatrefoil whilst another is octagonal. The chancel arch with renewed stiff-leaf corbels is only slightly later, and the unbuttressed west tower with lancets and a treble chambered east arch is 13th century. Of the 15th century are the tower battlements and pinnacles and the chancel windows, that on the east being straight-headed. There are shields on the chancel south wall. Inside are a small 14th century Italian painting of the Crucifixion and an effigy in sunk relief of a lady said to be Lady Furnival, and if so presumably brought from Worksop, where she was buried.

BARLOW   *St Laurence*   SK 344746

In 1867 S.Rollinson added a neo-Norman east end to a genuine Norman church comprised of nave and chancel. Both have plain original doorways, that in the small original chancel being blocked. The chancel has a late 13th century window and there is a late 16th or 17th century window in the nave. The south chapel has a five light window with ogival heads to the lights, probably 17th century. There is an incised slab to Robert Barley, d1467, and his wife Margaret.

BARROW-UPON-TRENT   *St Wilfred*   SK 353284

The restored mid 13th century north arcade has double chamfered arches and one piers is circular with four attached shafts with rings. The only unrestored window is that at the east end of the north aisle, with 14th century reticulated tracery. Also 14th century are the south arcade with octagonal piers and the lower part of the tower, the upper parts being 15th century. Both tower and clerestory were altered in the 19th century. There are squints from the aisles into the chancel. The alabaster effigy of a priest is 14th century.

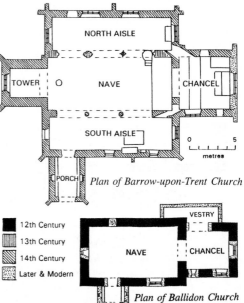

Plan of Barrow-upon-Trent Church

12th Century
13th Century
14th Century
Later & Modern

Plan of Ballidon Church

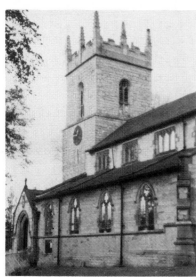

Barlborough Church

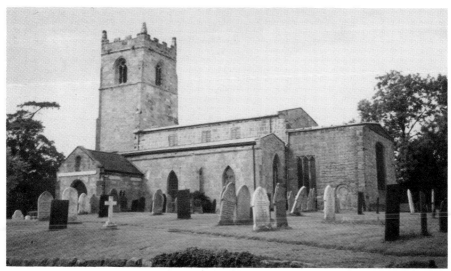

Barrow-upon-Trent Church

BARTON BLOUNT   *St Chad*   SK 208347

Now a private chapel serving the hall, this was once the parish church of a deserted village, some of the houses of which have been excavated. The chapel has a blocked north doorway which may be medieval but it was remodelled in 1714 by Samuel Taborer with pilasters and pinnacles at the corners and a large south doorway with a curly pediment. Lancets were inserted during a second remodelling in 1845.

BASLOW   *St Anne*   SK 252723

The odd positioning of the late 13th century tower beyond the west wall of the wide north aisle is probably because the aisle was originally the nave, although it could be a consequence of the positioning of the church close to the Derwent. The tower has angle buttresses and a broach spire with dormer windows between the broaches. The church itself is all embattled but was mostly rebuilt by Paxton for the Duke of Devonshire in the 1850s, whilst the chancel and vestry are of 1911. Until then the chancel had three Norman sedilia, possibly reset. The aisle roofs are 15th century. In the porch are a fragment of a Saxon cross shaft with interlace ornamentation and a coffin slab with a floriated cross and two keys, probably for a former steward of the two manors of Haddon and Baslow. Other slabs with a variety of vocational motifs are been re-used as the lintels of the 15th century clerestory windows. From 1718 until 1852 a minstrels gallery stood at the nave west end with an organ below. Near the south door are 18th century Royal Arms painted on canvas in a wooden frame.

BEELEY   *St Anne*   SK 265677

The south porch and north aisle and vestry are of the restoration of 1882-4 by H.Cockbain. Original are the Norman south doorway set (or reset) close the SW corner, parts of the chancel, and the west tower set against the southern two thirds of the west wall, both these being 14th century. There is a brass depicting John Calvert, d1710, in a shroud, this being one the latest figure brasses.

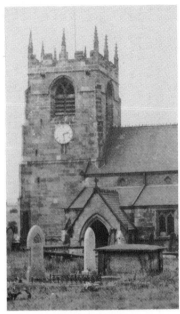

St John's Church, Belper

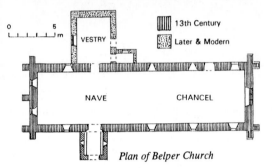

Beighton Church

Plan of Belper Church

BEIGHTON   *St Mary*   SK 443834

This church now lies in the built-up area of Sheffield. The tower with diagonal buttresses, battlements and eight pinnacles, and a tower arch with coarsely ornamented capitals is probably 16th century, the likely period also of the arcade with two wavy curves on the profile of the octagonal piers and arches.

BELPER   *St John the Baptist*   SK 352475

At The Butts lies the original chapel of the village before it developed into a textile town. The single chamber nave and chancel have small renewed 13th century lancets. It appears that there was once a date-stone of 1634 on the porch.

BIRCHOVER   *St Michael*   SK 236621

Below the cliff edge of Rowtor Rocks is a chapel erected by the Rev Thomas Eyre, d1717. It was remodelled and a chancel added c1869. Built into the porch-cum-vestry are Norman architectural fragments whose source of origin is unknown.

BLACKWELL   *St Werburgh*   SK 444584

A stump of a Saxon cross shaft lies in the churchyard. Of the medieval church the only relic is a single pier of c1190-1200 visible on the inner face of the north wall. The tower dates from a rebuilding of 1827-8 by Daniel Hodkin and the rest is the product of another rebuilding of 1878-9 by J.B.Mitchell-Withers.

BOLSOVER   *St Mary*   SK 474706

The church was mostly rebuilt to a design by Ambler after being gutted by fire in 1897. New roofs, dormers, and an octagonal vestry were added after another fire in 1960. Relics of the old church are the south doorway of the chancel with a treble roll-moulded frame and a defaced Crucifixion in the tympanum, the west tower, also 13th century, and the Cavendish Chapel added beyond the east end of the south aisle in 1624. The tower has broad angle buttresses, a west doorway with one order of columns, a lancet and two-light windows above, and a broach-spire with two tiers of dormers. There are foliated cross-slabs in the north porch and inside the church is a fine late relief carving of the Nativity. In the chapel is a splendid monument to Charles Cavendish, d1617, with his effigy above and behind that of his wife. There is an equally fine monument of 1727 with allegorical figures rather than effigies of the deceased to Henry Cavendish, Duke of Newcastle, his wife and one of his daughters. The monument features a large black sarcophagus between coupled Corinthian columns and was designed by Gibbs and sculpted by Francis Bird. Buried in the churchyard are the masons John and Huntingdon Smythson, died 1634 and 1648, who worked on rebuilding the castle.

Bolsover Church

BONSALL   *St James*   SK 280582

The embattled church lies on a hill above the village and the Bonsall Brook. Much of the exterior was rebuilt in 1862-3 by Ewan Christian but the chancel north wall and the three bay south arcade with quatrefoil piers with cables on the capitals are 13th century, the north arcade with octagonal piers is 14th century, and the tower is 15th century. It is ashlar faced with diagonal buttresses, pinnacles, battlements and a spire with two ornamental bands around it. In the north aisle is a 17th century funeral helmet and there is an oval wall-monument with weeping putti to Henry Ferne, d1763, and his wife and daughter.

BORROWASH   *St Stephen*   SK 418345

The church was entirely rebuilt in 1899 by P.H.Currey, but it contains a communion rail of the 1720s said to be from Hopwell Hall. It and a fine wrought iron screen given to the church by the Pares family are thought to be the work of Bakewell of Derby.

BOULTON   *St Mary*   SK 380325

The west end is of 1840 by John Mason, the north aisle was added in 1870, and the building was further enlarged c1960 by Sebastian Comper. Older relics are the Norman doorways in the chancel and nave, the latter with one order of colonettes and chevrons on the arch, some late medieval windows, and the south porch with a cusped outer entrance of c1300.

BOYLESTONE   *St John the Baptist*   SK 182358

The chancel with a finely moulded low recess in the north wall is early 14th century, and the south aisle windows and arcade are of the same period. The chancel east window is 15th century. According to an inscription the SW tower with a pyramidal roof with conical sides was built in 1844 to a design by Henry Duesbury.

BRACKENFIELD   *Holy Trinity*   SK 374590

The new church of 1856-7 designed by T.C.Hine, with a NE chapel and vestry added in 1872, contains a screen transferred from the 16th century Trinity chapel, now lying in ruins 1km to the NNW. The chapel has a four-light east window, plus three other windows and a doorway and porch on the south side.

BRADBOURNE   *All Saints*   SK 208528

In the churchyard is a Saxon cross-shaft of c1800 with a Crucifixion scene. The nave north wall is also partly Saxon and has long-and-short work at the NE corner. Both the nave and chancel have single 13th century north lancets, that in the chancel containing some old glass. The west tower is Norman and has doorways both to the west and south, although the latter, with one order of columns and voussiors with animals and also beakheads stylised into abstract tongue-shapes, may be the nave south doorway reset after the addition of the south aisle. The belfry windows have chevrons and billets and there is an original corbel table, the battlements being later. The low south arcade with keeled quatrefoil piers is of c1300. Of the late 14th century are the chancel arch with castellated responds and two windows in each of the south aisle and chancel. The only Victorian parts are the north vestry and the chancel SW window. There is an Italian early 17th century painting of the Adoration of the Shepherds, and in the south aisle is a 16th or 17th century wall painting with towers flanking an inscription from Ecclesiastes VI.

BRADLEY   *All Saints*   SK 224460

The nave and chancel are both 14th century, and there are two corbel-heads of that period set on either side of the inside of the east window. The 13th century font has an octagonal bowl with fleur-de-lis flanked by trefoil arches and a base formed of eight filleted shafts clustered together. The wooden bell-turret is 18th century.

BRADWELL   *St Barnabas*   SK 175811

The church is of 1867-8 by C.C.Townsend and has a tower added in 1888-91. It contains a pulpit and altar rail with early 18th century carved panels supposedly from a college chapel.

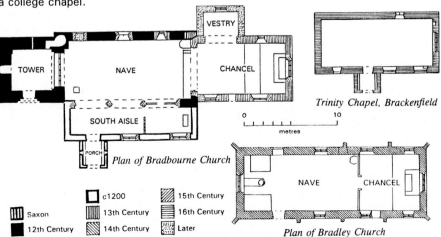

VESTRY

TOWER | NAVE | CHANCEL

SOUTH AISLE

PORCH

Plan of Bradbourne Church

Trinity Chapel, Brackenfield

0   10

metres

NAVE | CHANCEL

Plan of Bradley Church

c1200   15th Century
Saxon   13th Century   16th Century
12th Century   14th Century   Later

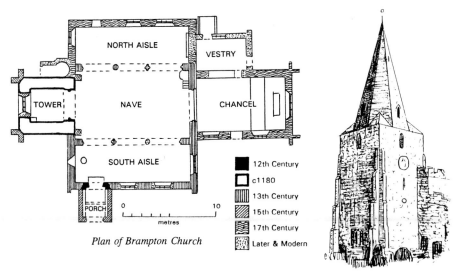

Plan of Brampton Church

■	12th Century
□	c1180
⊞	13th Century
▨	15th Century
▩	17th Century
▨	Later & Modern

Brampton Church

BRAILSFORD *All Saints* SK 245413

The church lies in trees away from the village. In the churchyard is a defaced stump of a Saxon cross shaft decorated with interlace and a human figure. The south arcade is Norman with scalloped capitals on the piers, one of which is octagonal and the other two circular but of differing sizes. The tower south wall lies flush with the arcade. The tower is ashlar faced with diagonal buttresses and a west doorway and window of the 15th century. The chancel is early 14th century with windows and sedilia and piscina typical of that period. On the south side of the chancel arch is a squint. The north side windows are 15th century but others of that period on the south side are renewed. There are bench ends with tracery panels and shields and the reredos includes linenfold panels of the 1520s and late gothic tracery panels.

BRAMPTON *St Peter and St Paul* SK 336719

The tower dates from the end of the 12th century and has an original south doorway and an arch to the nave with keeled responds and a pointed arch of three orders, only one of which is chamfered. A broach spire was added to it in the early years of the 13th century, and the angle buttresses were added then or later. Two other buttresses project into the nave. The nave south doorway is Norman, whilst the blocked north doorway is 13th century. The 13th century arcades of three bays have circular and quatrefoil shaped piers and the chancel arch matches them. In 1821 relieving arches were inserted and the east piers removed, but they were reinstated during the restoration by S.Rollinson in 1868, when the windows were mostly replaced. Of the 15th century are the clerestory, the battlements on the nave, south aisle, and chancel, and the vaulted south porch with massive transverse arches. In the south aisle walls are small figures of c1300 depicting St Peter and St Paul, The Angel and Virgin of the Annunciation, and a seated Christ. There is a slab to Matilda le Caus, d1224, showing her feet at the bottom and her upper half with hands holding a heart in a quatrefoil at the top. The monument to the Clarke family made in 1673 is very rustic. There is also a wall-monument to Geoffrey Clarke, d1734.

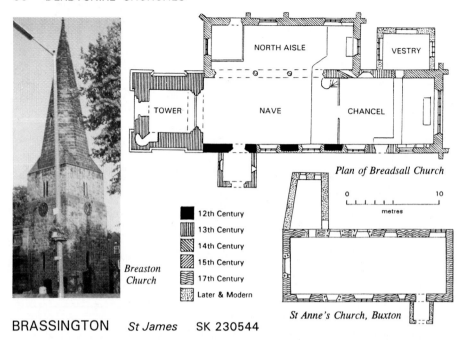

NORTH AISLE

VESTRY

TOWER

NAVE

CHANCEL

Plan of Breadsall Church

■ 12th Century

▥ 13th Century

▨ 14th Century

▧ 15th Century

▩ 17th Century

▒ Later & Modern

Breaston Church

0 _____ 10

metres

St Anne's Church, Buxton

BRASSINGTON   *St James*   SK 230544

The north aisle and vestry were built in 1879-81, designed by F.J.Robinson, and much of the exterior of the rest was rebuilt about the same time. However important Norman parts have survived in the form of an ashlar faced west tower with a blocked west doorway and two-light bell openings, the western part of the narrow south aisle, and the three bay south arcade with circular piers with waterleaf and multi-scalloped capitals. Inside the tower west wall is a figure of a naked man holding a heart. On the south side of the chancel is a narrow chapel with a two bay arcade of c1200 with an octagonal pier with a crocket capital and unmoulded arches. The south porch is late 13th century, but the inner doorway is 15th century, as were several windows before the rebuilding.

BREADSALL   *All Saints*   SK 371398

The church was extensively restored in 1915 by Caroe after being set on fire by suffragettes the previous year. It has a Norman south doorway with two orders of columns and chevrons on the arches. The chancel and north arcade are partly 13th century work, the arcade piers being circular with octagonal capitals decorated with nailheads. The sedilia in the chancel are late 14th century and have ogival heads and shields in the spandrels. The 13th century west tower is very fine and has at the lowest level a west doorway and a triple-chambered arch to the nave, above are two-light windows under hood-moulds, and then the bell-stage has pairs of large double chamfered lancets. The battlements and the lofty recessed spire were added in the early 14th century. The restored south windows are a late 14th century design, straight-headed with hood-moulds and reticulated tracery. The north aisle has a squint into the chancel and a mixture of early 14th century windows with cusped intersected tracery and later 14th century ones in the Perpendicular style. During an earlier restoration of 1877 a wooden late 14th century sculpture probably of German origin depicting the Pieta was discovered below the floor.

Plan of Caldwell Chapel

St Anne's Church, Buxton

BREASTON   *St Michael*   SK 460335

Much of the church is 13th century, the west tower being unbuttressed with a short broach spire and having a blocked 18th century doorway. The south aisle has a three bay arcade with double chamfered arches on octagonal piers and windows composed of three lancets with the middle one taller than the others. The chancel east window is early 14th century. The clerestory is late medieval. The NE vestry was added during a restoration by Evans and Jolly in 1895. The font is of 1720. A NW buttress with shields and initials is dated 1680.

BUXTON   *St Anne*   SK 057730

Hidden away behind the south end of the High Street is a humble chapel probably dating from 1625, the year that appears on a north porch which in its present form appears Victorian. The irregularly shaped SE vestry is also Victorian. The church itself is a single chamber with an irregular layout of plain rectangular windows, one on the north side being of three lights.

CALDWELL   *St Giles*   SK 254172

This is a much restored Norman chapel consisting of a nave and chancel with small round headed windows. The nave has a bellcote and a blocked round headed north doorway. In the west window are two roundels of stained glass probably of c1400. The north vestry and south porch are Victorian.

CALKE   *St Giles*   SK 369224

The church lies in the grounds of the mansion known as Calke Abbey and was rebuilt in 1826 with a narrow tower and embattled nave. It contains a fine monument to the builder of Calke Abbey, Sir John Harpur, d1741, and his wife.

CARSINGTON   *St Margaret*   SK 263534

The single embattled chamber with straight-headed three-light Perpendicular style windows seems to be later than it looks, since the sundial on the east wall has an inscription "Re-edified 1648". Of the 19th century are the pediment and bellcote at the west end and perhaps the east window with intersecting Y-tracery.

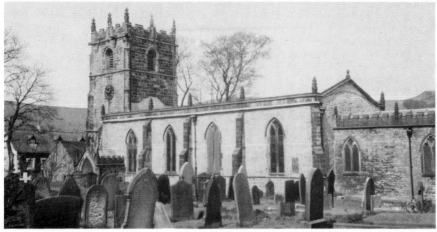

Castleton Church

CASTLETON   *St Edmund*   SK 150829

The chancel arch with chevrons and one order of colonettes is Norman. The chancel looks small enough to be Norman also but the quoins of the east corners look as if they are the same period as the ashlar-faced 15th century west tower with diagonal buttresses, battlements and eight pinnacles. The nave is wide and long with the proportions one might expect in a Norman church with an important castle nearby. However the existing walling is mostly of 1837, when later medieval aisles were removed. There are a fine set of box pews dated 1661, 1662, 1663 and 1676.

CHADDESDEN   *St Mary*   SK 382369

Much of the church dates from a rebuilding in the 1350s by Henry Chaddesden, Archdeacon of Leicester, who established a college or chantry here. The spacious chancel with three light windows with a star motif in the tracery, and the aisles with three bay arcades with tall octagonal piers are of that date. Some of the windows were replaced in the 15th century when the aisles were extended to the west and an ashlar faced tower with angle buttresses was added. Each aisle has sedilia and a piscina at the east end. The chancel has a bible rest built into the north wall. The east window dates from a restoration of 1857 by G.Place, and in the following year Street worked on the nave and aisles, changing the tracery in some of the windows. There is an old screen and there are stall ends with figures of a monk and a deacon.

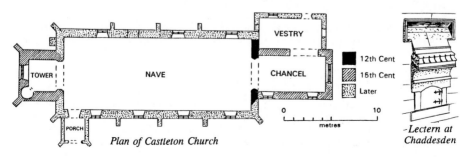

Plan of Castleton Church

-Lectern at Chaddesden

CHAPEL-EN-LE-FRITH   *St Thomas Becket*   SK 058808

A Saxon cross-shaft lies in the churchyard but the earliest church here is said to have been built in 1225 by the foresters of Peak Forest (the name means Chapel-in-the-Forest). The existing nave and aisles of four bays with octagonal sandstone piers with nailhead decoration on the south side, and the chancel and chancel arch are all early 14th century. However the chancel was remodelled in the 1890s by Darbyshire & Smith, when vestries were added on either side of it, and the south side of the church was made Georgian with round arch windows and pilaster buttresses in the 1730s by G.Platt. The west tower with obelisk pinnacles also now looks Georgian, although much of the walling seems to be medieval. Extensive modern vestries and meeting rooms flank the tower north side and much of the north aisle. There are early 19th century box pews. The font is 15th century, there are altar rails of 1681 now at the west end, and there is a chandelier of 1731.

CHELLASTON   *St Peter*   SK 381304

The small church is probably mostly late 13th century, the south aisle having a three bay arcade with octagonal arcades and an east window with intersecting tracery. The chancel is later medieval and the west tower was rebuilt in 1842. Inside are a Norman font and an incised slab to John Bancroft, d1557, and his wife.

CHELMORTON   *St John the Baptist*   SK 115704

The earliest part is the three bay south arcade of c1200 with octagonal piers and double-chamfered arches. When the north aisle and its four bay arcade were added towards the end of the 13th century the south arcade was given an extra east arch which opens into a transept which projects east beyond the chancel arch. The transept has typical late 13th century windows, with three stepped lancets facing south and a two-light window with a pierced spandrel to the east. Refacing has removed the external opening of a north doorway with a steeply pointed trefoiled head of c1300 and any traces of former end windows in the aisle. The sedilia and piscina suggest a mid 14th century date for the chancel, and the tower with angle buttresses and a NW stair turret is of the same period. Of the 15th century are the altered clerestory above the south arcade, the porch, the octagonal font, and the low embattled stone rood screen with an ogee-arcade and openwork quatrefoils above. There is a Baroque tablet to George Dale, d1683.

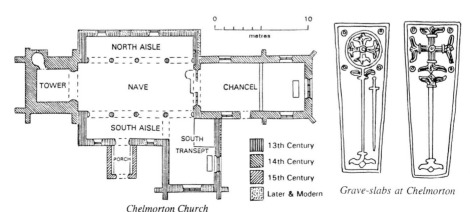

Chelmorton Church

Grave-slabs at Chelmorton

CHESTERFIELD   *St Mary and All Saints*   SK 385712

This is a large church mostly of c1325-50 with an aisled nave of six bays, a central tower, transepts, and a two bay chancel flanked by a chapel of St Katherine on the north and by a Lady Chapel on the south. Beyond the Lady Chapel is a feature unusual in an English parish church, another chapel (lesser Lady Chapel) with a polygonal east end. There is a rectangular chapel of the Holy Cross in a corresponding position off the north transept, with a vestry added in 1963 east of it. The many chapels are due to the numerous guilds which existed in the town, the earliest of which, the Guild of Our Lady and the Holy Cross, being founded in 1218.

The trefoiled piscina in the Holy Cross chapel and the treble-chamfered crossing arches and south transept are relics of a 13th century church, a dedication being recorded in 1234. The transept originally had an east aisle (of which the arcade survives) before the present arrangement of chapels was created. The aisle windows are of three lights with typical Decorated style tracery, and the west window is of seven lights with flowing tracery, a transom and reticulation on each side. The west and north doorways, the south transept doorway, and the east window date from the restoration of 1843 by Gilbert Scott. The nave arcades have quatrefoil shaped piers with hollows in the diagonals and fillets on the main shafts. The capitals are moulded and the arches have two wavy mouldings. The south doorway with filleted shafts and a complex moulded arch lies in the western bay and has a porch in front of it.

The Lesser Lady Chapel has tall slim two-light windows and a piscina with an ogival trefoiled head. The Lady Chapel has three-light windows with reticulated tracery. The north transept was rebuilt in 1769 and given a pediment and a doorway below with its own pediment. There are 15th century windows in the clerestory, the west walls of the aisles, and in the east ends of the chancel chapels. The tower has pairs of two-light windows at the belfry stage and has a plain parapet, within which is a spire rising to 68m. The wooden frame of the spire has twisted so that it leans 3m to the SW. The lead plates covering the frame are laid herringbone fashion so the eight sides appear channelled but they are in fact flat.

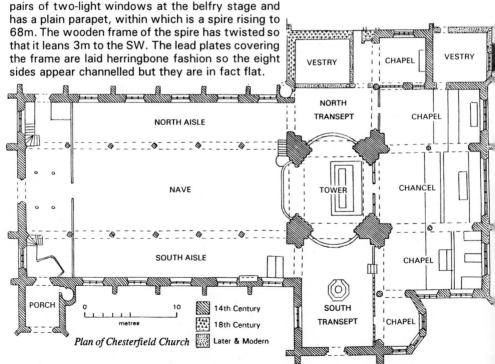

Plan of Chesterfield Church

14th Century
18th Century
Later & Modern

The tub-shaped font with leaf decoration and a foliated cross is Norman. The fine Jacobean pulpit may have been executed by the carvers of the long gallery at Haddon Hall. The original rood screen of c1475 from the chancel arch now closes off St Katherine's Chapel. The south transept has a screen of c1500, and between the Holy Cross Chapel and the choir vestry is a screen which originally belonged to the Foljambe Chapel of 1503-4. The fine two tier candelabrum in the Lady Chapel was presented to the church in 1760 and was originally hung in the nave. A processional cross is thought to be early 16th century Italian work. The stained glass in the various chapels and nave west window is 19th and 20th century work.

Under an ogival-headed and crocketed recess in the south aisle is an early 14th century effigy of a priest with his head on a pillow flanked by angels. In the Lady Chapel are many Foljambe monuments. A fine tomb chest made at Burton-on-Trent by the carvers Harper and Moorecock bears brasses depicting Henry, d1510, and his wife. The kneeling figure of a boy on top of this is probably Sir Thomas, d1604. The brasses of Sir Godfrey, d1529, and his wife have been renewed. There are fine recumbent effigies on a tomb chest of Sir Godfrey, d1585, and his wife. The incised alabaster slab to George, d1588, is damaged. The big standing wall-monument with recumbent effigies, dated 1592 on a framed panel, was erected in the lifetime of Godfrey and his wife, d1594. Godfrey also had erected the large tablet with the kneeling figure of Sir James Foljambe, d1558, and another mysterious monument with an effigy in a shroud now without any inscription surviving. A tablet to Godfrey Heathcote, d1773, signed by the Fishers, elder and younger, of York. Other tablets are to Mary Boucher, d1791, by Stead, and Elizabeth Bapshaw, d1792, by Blagden.

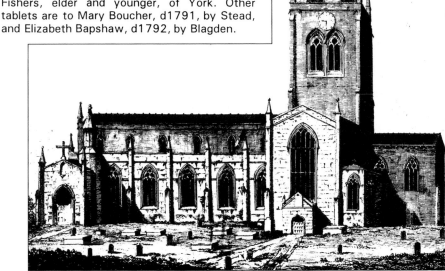

Old Print of Chesterfield Church

CHURCH BROUGHTON   *St Michael*   SK 205338

Relics of the Norman period are the font with a chevron motif with large intersecting circles, and the east respond of the north arcade with a scalloped capital. The rectangular pier with a demi-caryatid may be nearly as early and the aisle end windows are perhaps of c1300. The lower parts of the tower with angle buttresses, the south aisle with its doorway and windows, and the chancel with typical sedilia and piscina are all early 14th century. The 15th century clerestory and roof were altered in the 18th century, and the top is 19th century.

CHURCH GRESLEY   *St George and St Mary*   SK 293181

The 14th century north transeptal tower is a relic of an Augustinian priory founded here in the early 12th century and has a blocked treble-chamfered arch in its east wall. Except for the north arcade with octagonal piers and treble-chamfered arches the rest of the church, including the tower top, was rebuilt c1820. A new chancel was built in 1872 to a design by A.W.Blomfield. The fine mid-17th century stalls with miserichords in the chancel and at the west end have come from Drakelowe Hall.

CLOWNE   *St John the Baptist*   SK 498754

Both the nave and chancel are Norman (although the latter was rebuilt in 1955) and they are connected by an arch on imposts with three shafts. The arch beside the chancel arch probably once contained an altar. The nave south doorway has a roll-moulded arch and an order of columns with spiral motifs on the capitals. The doorway must be reset for there was once a south aisle. The chancel also has an original south doorway. There is a large lancet on the south side and the east window is 15th century. An altarpiece dated 1724 and signed by Bouttats of Antwerp has panels with Commandments, the Creed, Lord's Prayer and the Ascension.

CODNOR   *St James*   SK 419488

A medieval font found in the castle grounds lies in the church, which was rebuilt in 1843 with a thin west tower and a west gallery on iron columns. The chancel was added in 1888-90 to a design by J.Holden.

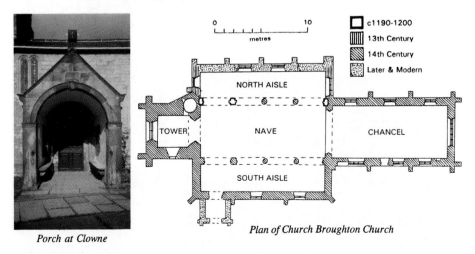

Porch at Clowne

Plan of Church Broughton Church

Norman arcade at Crich

CRICH   *St Michael*   SK 348547

The north arcade of three bays with circular piers, responds with scalloped capitals, and round unchamfered arches of two orders is Norman, as is the plain font. The south arcade with more detail on the capitals and single chamfered arches is also Norman but later, say c1180 as opposed to the 1130s or 40s. At the east end narrower pointed arches connect these arcades to the 14th century chancel with plain ogee-headed sedilia and renewed reticulated window tracery. In the chancel north wall is a rare stone bible rest. The aisle windows are a mixture of 14th and 15th century forms. The 15th century west tower has angle buttresses, a fine parapet with a wavy band with trefoils and a recessed spire with two tiers of dormer windows. There are two medieval bench ends with poppy-heads. One of several recesses in the north aisle wall contains a fine late 14th century effigy of a man in the gown which is assumed to be Sir William de Wakebridge, d1369. In the chancel is an effigy of Godfrey Beresford, d1513, an incised slab to German Pole, d1588 and his wife, and a incised slab on a tomb-chest to John Claye, d1632, and his two wives. There is also a tiny brass with a portrait of baby Ephraim Shelmardine, d1637.

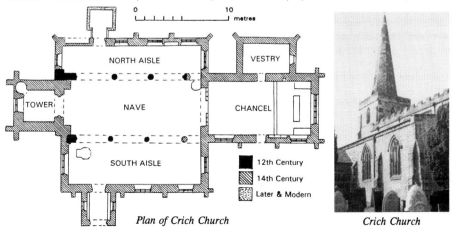

Plan of Crich Church   *Crich Church*

Cubley Church

Interior of Dale Abbey Church

CUBLEY   *St Andrew*   SK 165376

The plain font and the south arcade with circular piers and unchamfered arches are Norman. The 13th century chancel has a five-light east window which was restored by St Aubyn in 1872. The window contains fragments of 14th century glass with figures. The nave and south aisle have 17th century windows with a single mullion and transom, those in the nave being larger than the others. The early 16th century west tower has angle buttresses, a tall tower arch, and a large west doorway with a big window above it. The defaced effigy of Sir Nicholas Montgomery, d1494, on an alabaster tomb chest is thought to be the work of the carvers Harper and Morrecock, whose workshops were at Burton-on-Trent.

DALBURY   *All Saints*   SK 264343

The small church has an embattled bellcote and lancets, all of which are shown on drawings of the 1820s. One tiny lancet on the south contains medieval glass showing St Michael. A north aisle was added in 1849. Inside are a complete set of box-pews, a font with a 17th or 18th century cover, and an early 19th century organ case.

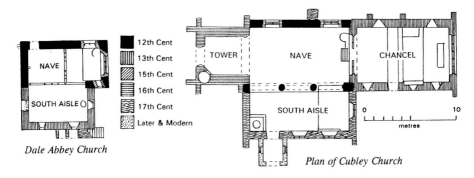

12th Cent
13th Cent
15th Cent
16th Cent
17th Cent
Later & Modern

NAVE

SOUTH AISLE

Dale Abbey Church

TOWER   NAVE   CHANCEL

SOUTH AISLE

0   10
metres

Plan of Cubley Church

DALE ABBEY   *All Saints*   SK 437386

It is likely that the nave with its Norman masonry represents the Chapel of Depedale mentioned in that period, whilst the south aisle is probably a late 13th century addition. The windows and the upper storey with its open timber roof housing a gallery are late medieval. The chapel adjoins a farmhouse with a roof common to both. The adjoining building is thought to have been used as an infirmary for the adjacent Premonstratension abbey from c1485 it was dissolved in 1538. This part has been rebuilt. At one time it was an inn called the Blue Bell within which clergy put on their robes before entering through a doorway blocked up c1820. The church ranked as a "peculiar" not under the authority of a bishop. When when the effects of the abbey were sold the rights of a bishop here passed to the new owner, Lord Stanhope. A tablet in the church describes one of the lords as "Lay Bishop of Dale". The interior is of much interest, being filled with box pews and a gallery. Apart from the installation of electricity little has changed since Cromwell's day. There is a pulpit of 1634 and the altar is fitted with drawers and shelves for storing communion plate. There is a defaced incised slab and on the north wall are late 13th century mural paintings of the Annunciation, the Visitation and the Nativity.

Dale Abbey Church

Darley Dale Church

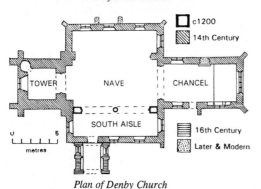

Plan of Denby Church

DARLEY DALE   *St Helen*

SK 267630

The church is cruciform and much of it is of 13th century origin, the south transept having east lancets, the chancel one south lancet, and the north arcade having three double-chamfered arches on circular piers. The south arcade with octagonal piers and the tall three-light end windows of the transepts are 14th century. The five light east window, the battlements of the nave and transepts, the nave roof with bosses and the west tower with head label stops to the west doorway and window are all 15th century. The north aisle and much of the south aisle were rebuilt in 1854 by Stevens. There is a small Norman font with ribbed edges and another of the later medieval period. The south aisle has a stone late medieval screen. The fragment of a Saxon cross-shaft with geometrical ornamentation was discovered in the 1950s. There are several foliated cross-slabs and there are incised slabs to John Rollesley, d1513, and his wife, and to John Rollesley, d1535, and his wife, plus another in a poor condition. There is also an effigy of a cross-legged knight of c1330 holding his heart in his hand, probably representing Sir John de Darley.

DENBY   *St Mary*   SK 399465

One respond of the two bay south arcade of c1200 has nailhead decoration. The chancel with a three-light east window and two-light side windows, and the west tower with angle buttresses connected at the top by a horizontal band and with a broach spire rising within a parapet with pierced pointed trefoils are 14th century. Several windows in the aisles appear to be of that period, but the north aisle seems to have been rebuilt in 1838 when the 15th century arcade was removed and a gallery inserted. The font may be formed from part of the former arcade pier. The 16th century south porch is not on the same axis as the south doorway. It is vaulted and has shafts subdividing the side walls into two panels. J Oldrid Scott restored the church in 1901-3.

DERBY *All Saints* SK 352365

There was a major religious establishment here in Saxon times, and Domesday Book in 1087 records King William as patron of a church served by a college of seven priests under the Dean of Lincoln. A sub-dean and the other priests lived in College Place north of the church. Nothing survives of major rebuilding in the 14th century and a tower of that period was demolished to make way for a larger new tower begun by 1520 and completed in 1532, the mason being John Otes. This edifice, one of the biggest of its type in Britain, still dominates the skyline of the town, being 63m high to the top of the huge pinnacles. There are bold buttresses slightly set back from the angles and a wide west doorway. The next stage has large blank three-light windows with four centred heads and blank niches. The bell-stage above has four-light windows with panel tracery. The battlements have blank tracery. Nine of the bells are 17th century, but the tenor is 15th century, i.e. older than the present tower. A church of St Mary not far to the west was demolished in medieval times.

In 1723 The main body of All Saints was summarily demolished on the orders of the then vicar, Dr Michael Hutchinson, after a dispute with the Corporation, who were responsible for the chancel and refused to pay for a rebuilding. By the time the Mayor realised what was happening it was too late. The present Classical style building of six bays was then erected by William (d1724) and Francis Smith of Warwick to a design by James Gibbs. It has large round headed windows divided by pilaster buttresses and a balustrade. There is intermittent rustication around the windows and doorways, a typical Gibbs' motif. The interior has Tuscan columns on tall bases allowing for former box pews. The aisles have groin-vaults and the nave a tunnel vault into which the arcade arches cut. Gibbs' furnishings were removed in the restoration of 1873-4 by J.Young. In 1927 the church was raised to the status of a cathedral and plans put in hand for a new east end. In the event the war delayed the work and Gibbs' Venetian east window and big pediment across both nave and aisles survived until 1967, when a two bay retrochoir with a shallow V-shaped apse was added to a design by Sebastian Comper. There are vestries flanking the retrochoir and meeting rooms underneath it.

Old view of the interior of All Saints' Church, now Derby Cathedral.

Tomb of Bess of Hardwick

All Saints' Church, Derby

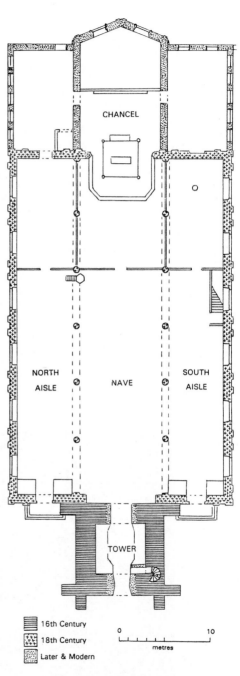

Plan of All Saints' Church, Derby

Many of the furnishings are 19th and 20th century. Older relics include the west gallery of 1732-3 on fluted Ionic columns, extended into the aisles in 1841, the 17th century panelling and raised seat in the north chancel chapel, an 18th century Bishop's throne from Constantinople, a richly carved 18th century Flemish cupboard in the NW corner, and the chancel screen, communion rails, and the stands for the mace and sword in the Corporation pew all by local smith Robert Bakewell, d1752.

In the north chapel is an alabaster slab of c1480 depicting Sub-Dean Lawe under a canopy with other figures. In the south chapel is a wall-monument with an effigy of the celebrated Elizabeth, Countess of Shrewsbury, better known as Bess of Hardwick. She lived until 1607 but by 1601 the monument was complete "and wanteth nothing but setting up". She had acquired what was then known as St Katherine's chapel in 1556 to be her burial place. Mounted coffin plates record the burial of over forty members of the Cavendish family in a vault below the chapel between 1607 and 1848. The chapel also contains a timber monument to Sub-Dean Robert Johnson, d1527. In the north aisle is a wall-monument with a kneeling figure of Richard Crowshawe, d1631. Another monument to William Allestry, d1655, and his wife, d1638, has a sarcophagus and four columns, while that of Sir William Wheeler, d1666, has two busts high up. Roubiliac designed the monument with busts of Thomas Chambers, d1726, and his wife. The many other 18th and 19th century monuments include those to Sarah Ballidon, d1734, Caroline, Countess of Bessborough, d1760, and a bust of William Ponsonby, Earl of Bessborough, d1793.

DERBY   *St Alkmund*   SK 352368

A church of 1846 by H.I.Stevens was demolished in 1967 to make room for the inner ring road. Excavations in 1968 revealed remains of a Saxon nave 13m long by 5.7m long not later than the 9th century. It had a chancel 5m square externally to the east and small transeptal chapels on either side of the nave east end. The church was extended to the east in the 12th century and provided with aisles. The south aisle was widened a century or so later, and the north aisle was remodelled and then extended to the west in the 15th century. A 9th century sarcophagus, possibly the tomb of St Alkmund, and other Saxon fragments were taken to the Derby Museum.

A 14th century font and an alabaster effigy of John Bullock, d1667, lie in the new church of St Alkmund in Kedleston Road, built 1967-72.

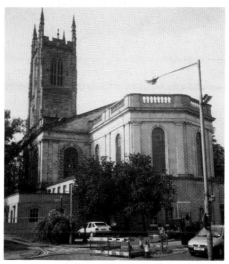

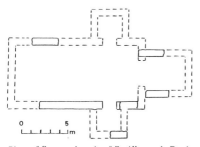

Plan of Saxon church of St Alkmund, Derby

All Saints' Church, Derby

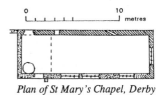

Plan of St Mary's Chapel, Derby

DERBY   *St Mary*   SK 354368

This is a rare surviving example of a medieval chapel built on a bridge. It is of 14th century origin but the east window is later medieval and has a half-timbered gable above. There is evidence of later repairs in brick. The springing of the first arch of the old bridge can be seen below the east end. Inside is a tiny gallery. Since the Reformation the building has been used as a dwelling and warehouse but it was restored as a chapel in 1931 thanks to the Derby Archaeological Society and the Haslam family. The present south windows and most of the roof beams are of that date. On the north side is a squint allowing a view of the altar from a former hermitage there.

DERBY   *St Michael*   SK 352367

The existing church, now used as an office, dates from 1857, the east end of the medieval church having fallen the previous year. An old picture shows it as having a south aisle flanking both the nave and west tower, and a south porch. The tower top and one of the windows are shown in 15th century style.

Bridge Chapel of St Mary, Derby

DERBY   *St Peter*   SK 353360

The east wall of the nave and the responds of the arcades with scalloped capitals are Norman. The arcade piers, circular on the north, and octagonal on the south, are not much later. There was considerable rebuilding in the 14th century, five-light windows of that date remaining in the south aisle, and other more modest ones in the north aisle and the west part of the chancel. A two storey NE vestry added at the end of that century was rebuilt in 1865. The chancel was restored by G.G.Place in 1851-3, and in 1859 G.E. Street restored the rest. He removed the 18th century pews and galleries. A medieval traceried chest is the only ancient furnishing to survive. In 1898 the west tower was rebuilt and the nave extended by one bay.

St Peter's Church, Derby

DERBY   *St Werburgh*   SK 350364

The tower with obelisk pinnacles dates from 1601, replacing a 15th century tower which had collapsed. The rest was rebuilt in 1699 but only the chancel survived another rebuilding in 1892-4 by Sir Arthur Blomfield in which the orientation was changed so that the altar lay on the north with the old chancel as a long side chapel. It retains a fine reredos of 1708 by Henry Huss with carved Royal Arms above. The church is now shut up, but contained shops until recently. The wrought iron font cover of 1716 is by Bakewell. There are many monumental wall-tablets. Dr Johnson was married to the much older Elizabeth Porter in this church in 1735.

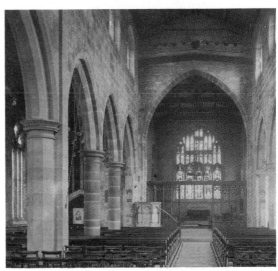

St Werburgh's Church, Derby   *Interior of St Peter's Church, Derby*

DETHICK   *St John the Baptist*   SK 327579

The church lies on a hill and has a fine west tower dated 1530 and paid for by Sir Anthony Babington. It has diagonal buttresses and a tall polygonal SE stair turret. Below the bell-openings is a frieze of shields of Sir Anthony and his kinsmen. There are battlements and eight pinnacles at the top. The tower arch is comparatively narrow. The main body of the church is 13th century, as evidenced by two lancets. There is no chancel arch, but a clerestory was added later.

DOVERIDGE   *St Cuthbert*   SK 114341

The fine 13th century chancel still has five long lancets on the north side, and three plus a roll-moulded doorway on the south. The tower with clasping buttresses is also 13th century with narrow lancets in the lowest stage and coupled lancets with dogtooth decoration and hood-moulds above. The top stage and the spire recessed behind an embattled parapet are probably 14th century, the period of the aisles with flowing and reticulated tracery in the windows. The clerestory and the five light east window are 15th century. The absence of a chancel arch or much stained glass makes for a very light interior. There are however some fragments of medieval glass in the SW window. The incised alabaster slab to a priest is probably 14th century. There is an incised slab with a brass surround in front of a wall recess to Ralph Okeover, d1487. There are also wall-monuments to William Davenport, d1640, and his wife, and Thomas Milward, d1658.

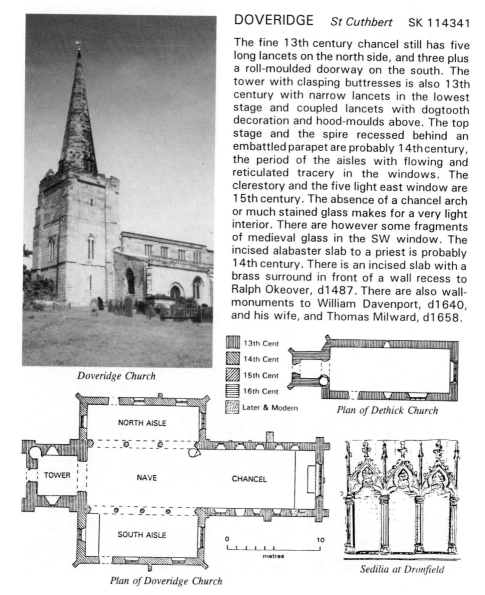

Doveridge Church

- ▨ 13th Cent
- ▧ 14th Cent
- ▨ 15th Cent
- ▤ 16th Cent
- ▒ Later & Modern

Plan of Dethick Church

NORTH AISLE

TOWER   NAVE   CHANCEL

SOUTH AISLE

0   10
metres

Plan of Doveridge Church

Sedilia at Dronfield

DRONFIELD   *St John the Baptist*   SK 353784

The nave, originally Saxon or Norman, is comparatively narrow and once had a steep roof. The west tower and spire are 15th century, although the tower arch goes with the aisles and the fine chancel which are of the first half of the 14th century. In both the chancel and south aisle are windows with intersecting tracery with a quatrefoil at the top. The aisles have squints into the chancel. The sedilia in the chancel have thin filletted shafts and thickly crocketed ogees and gables, the arches being double cusped with small figures. The piscina with ogee tracery is separate. Two chancel windows and one in the nave have fragments of their original stained glass. The original tracery of the seven light east window fell out in 1563 and there are now only plain mullions and transoms. There is a fine Jacobean pulpit with knobs on the columns. A brass of 1399 has effigies of the priests Thomas and Richard Gomfrey. There are also brasses of John Fanshawe, d1580, and his wife and family, and several brass inscriptions in the chancel floor. There is a mid 15th century alabaster effigy of Sir Richard Barley on a tomb chest with angels holding shields.

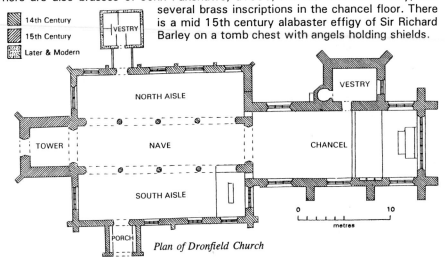

Plan of Dronfield Church

Dronfield Church

Duffield Church

DUFFIELD   *St Alkmund*   SK 350428

The early 14th century west tower has angle buttresses connected on top by a horizontal band below the battlements and a recessed spire, upon which is a weathercock of 1719 by Bakewell. The north transept is slightly earlier, having an end window with three stepped lancets. The chancel has a five light 15th century east window with panel tracery. The ogee-arched recess in the north wall and several windows are 14th century but the masonry is probably 13th century. The other windows are straight-headed, those in the south aisle being of the time of the restoration of 1846 by St Aubyn, or that by J.Oldrid Scott in 1896. The three bay arcades are of uncertain date. That on the north looks the earliest (late 13th century?) but could be a 17th century replacement. On a tomb chest are the alabaster effigies of Sir Roger Mynors, d1539, and his wife. There is also a wall-monument with small figures upon a frieze depicting Anthony Bradshaw, d1614 and his two wives, four sons, and sixteen daughters.

EARL STERNDALE   *St Michael*   SK 081671

In the church of 1828 by G.E.Hamilton with a chancel of 1877 by R.R.Duke, rebuilt in 1950 after war damage, is a font which is probably early 12th century.

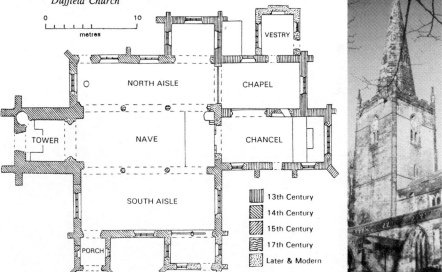

0 — 10 metres

NORTH AISLE   CHAPEL

VESTRY

TOWER   NAVE   CHANCEL

SOUTH AISLE

PORCH

▦ 13th Century
▨ 14th Century
▧ 15th Century
▤ 17th Century
▦ Later & Modern

Tower at Dronfield

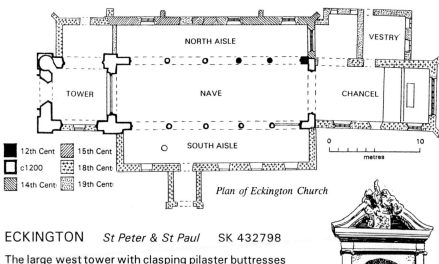

Plan of Eckington Church

- ■ 12th Cent
- ☐ c1200
- ▨ 14th Cent
- ▨ 15th Cent
- ▦ 18th Cent
- ▦ 19th Cent

ECKINGTON   *St Peter & St Paul*   SK 432798

The large west tower with clasping pilaster buttresses
and three lancets on each side at the bell-stage was
begun c1200. The tower arch has keeled responds.
The spire recessed behind a parapet is probably 14th
century. When the tower was added two extra bays
with octagonal piers were added to three bay arcades
of c1185-1200, the northern side being a little earlier
than the southern, and the chancel arch is of the
same date. The eastern part of the north aisle outer
wall is 14th century, the west end and the clerestory
being 15th century. The south aisle and porch belong
to a remodelling of 1763 by John Platt, the windows
being round arched and the porch heavily rusticated.
The south aisle west end was rebuilt in 1802. The
chancel was also rebuilt, only to be gothicized again
in 1907. The communion rail with foliated balusters is
early 18th century. The earliest of several memorials
to the Sitwell family is that to Margaret, d1658.

Tablet at Eckington

EDENSOR   *St Peter*   SK 251699

This is essentially a proud estate church of 1867 by
Sir George Gilbert Scott for the sixth Duke of
Devonshire, but four of the arcade piers are original
13th century work, and in the 15th century south
porch are some loose stones from the Norman church
and a foliated cross-slab. In the chapel at the east end
of the south aisle is a huge monument to William, first
Earl of Devonshire, d1625, and Henry Cavendish,
d1616. Under a four-posted canopy Henry is depicted
as a skeleton on a straw mat whilst William lies in a
shroud but with his face exposed. There is a brass to
John Beton, d1570, servant of Mary, Queen of Scots.
Joseph Paxton was buried here in 1865.

Eckington Church

EDLASTON *St James* SK 181426

The small church has a casual grouping of straight-headed windows on the south side. The chancel is 14th century with an east window of c1870. The double bellcote is of 1900 by E.Arden Minty.

EGGINTON *St Wilfrid* SK 265285

Much of the small church is of c1300, notably the west tower with its bell-openings, the chancel with trefoil headed sedilia and piscina and typical windows, plus the aisles with their arcades with circular piers on the north but quatrefoil ones on the south. There is a series of recesses in the south aisle south wall, in which is also a 16th century window. The tower west window is 15th century. The church was restored in 1891 by Evans and Jolly. There are fragments of 13th century glass depicting the Virgin, St John, and the Crucifixion. There is a very damaged effigy of a medieval civilian holding his heart in his hands and there is a black medallion with a white frontal bust to Francis Every, d1690.

ELMTON *St Peter* SK 503734

As rebuilt in 1773 the church comprises a nave and a lower apsed chancel plus an incomplete west tower. The windows are arched. There are none facing north. Of the period of the church is the pulpit and tester.

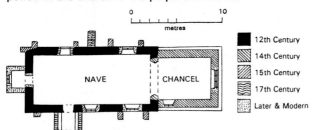

0   10
metres

■ 12th Century
▨ 14th Century
▨ 15th Century
▤ 17th Century
▦ Later & Modern

NAVE   CHANCEL

Plan of Edlaston Church

Incised slab at Etwall

Egginton Church

ELTON   *All Saints*   SK 222610

The font is a replica of that taken to Youlgreave in 1838. Elton was a chapel-of-ease to Youlgreave until that year. The church has a tower with a broach spire and a south aisle but was entirely rebuilt in 1812.

ELVASTON   *St Bartholomew*   SK 406330

The church, once dedicated to St Mary, lies near Elvaston Castle in grounds now forming a country park. The chancel is of c1200 but was restored and extended by Bodley in 1904-5. The late 13th century south aisle has a three bay arcade with octagonal piers carrying double chamfered-arches, a west lancet, and south windows with intersecting tracery. The nave north windows with straight-sided arches and the clerestory are probably works undertaken in accordance with the 1474 will of Lord Mountjoy of Elvaston. The tower with angle buttresses and tall twin two-light bell-openings under single ogival arches is also 15th century. A wall-monument has alabaster effigies of Sir John Stanhope, d1610, and his wife. There is a tablet with a brass inscription to the plasterer William Piggin, d1621. In a transeptal extension with a tall mullioned and transomed window lie fragments of a monument to Sir John Stanhope, d1638, which were reassembled in 1731. Among several 19th century monuments are those of the third and fifth Earls of Harrington.

ETWALL   *St Helen*   SK 268320

The church lies between a row of almshouses and the village street. It has a short diagonally buttressed west tower probably of c1300-50. The low main body has windows of late medieval type although those on the south may actually be late 17th or 18th century. The round-headed south doorway containing a fine 17th century door is 13th century, and the three bay arcade is Norman work with circular piers with scalloped capitals and arches without mouldings or chamfers. There is a taller, wider and later fourth arch which is pointed and double chamfered. An incised slab to an early 16th century civilian and his wife is badly damaged. Brasses remain of the wife and children of Henry Port, d1512, his figure being lost. In a finely carved straight-topped recess in the chancel south wall are brasses of Sir John Port, d1557, and his wife and children. A tomb-chest top has effigies in sunk relief with a band across the bodies of a man assumed to be Sir John Port, d1541 and his two wives.

Elvaston Church

Eyam Church

Saxon cross at Eyam

EYAM *St Lawrence* SK 218765

Of the 13th century are the chancel with lancet windows and the north arcade of three bays with one circular pier and one which is a keeled quatrefoil, the arches being double chamfered, although one chamfer is slight. The south arcade with octagonal piers and the clerestory and nave roof look 15th century. So does the west tower, although the tower arch is probably 14th century and much of the rest is of a rebuilding commemorated by a 1618 datestone. The north aisle and chancel were restored by Street in 1868-9, and the south aisle and porch were rebuilt by J.D.Webster in 1882-3. Between the clerestory windows are six cartouches of a series with the signs of the twelve tribes of Israel, originally painted in Elizabethan times but later gone over again. Over the chancel arch is part of a Creed from a scheme of 1645. the Norman font has blank arches on columns. Elizabethan parts from the former Stafford Pew are reused in the screens to the chancel and tower. William Montpesson, who shut Eyam off from the outer world in 1666 after the plague was brought in from London, and then ministered to the dying, holding open air services, is commemorated by a chair with a crude figure of the Virgin above which is the inscription Mon 1665 Eyam. His wife was among the victims. In the churchyard is a 9th century Saxon cross, lacking part of the shaft decorated with vine scrolls and interlace but unusually retaining the head with defaced figures.

Fenny Bentley Church

FENNY BENTLEY   *St Edmund*   SK 175502

The nave and chancel are divided only by an early 16th century screen. Another old screen divided the north aisle of 1847-50 by Stevens from the Beresford Chapel rebuilt about the same time. Also rebuilt is the west tower, to which a spire was added in 1864. The nave is Norman and retains an original south doorway, now with a small 14th century porch in front. The chancel is of c1300 with a five-light window with unusual tracery. Under an arcade between the chancel and chapel is a tomb chest with effigies of Thomas Beresford, d1473, and his wife. The monument was made about a century later and the problem of no likeness of the deceased being available was solved by depicting them bundled up in burial shrouds. The children around the tomb chest sides are shown in the same way.

FINDERN   *All Saints*   SK 309305

Only a Norman tympanum with figures and crosses, a font of 1662, and an incised slab to Isabella de Fynderne, d1444, survived a total rebuilding in 1863-4.

FOREMARK   *St Saviour*   SK 329265

At a glance the church looks medieval but it was in fact built in 1662 by Sir Francis Burdett. The symmetrical south front with a single five-light window without tracery on either side of a central buttress and the square stops of the hood-moulds betray the real date. The aisleless nave and tower are both embattled. The interior has box-pews, a fine contemporary screen and a three-decker pulpit, and there are iron altar-rails of c1710 by Bakewell.

GLOSSOP   *All Saints*   SK 042948

The west tower is of 1853, the nave is of 1914-15 by C.M.Hadfield, and the chancel (also by Hadfield) is of 1923. The only medieval relics are a pair of head corbels supporting an arch not originally upon them at the north aisle east end.

Great Longstone Church

GREAT LONGSTONE   *St Giles*   SK 200719

The lancets in the north aisle and the south doorway may be 13th century. The six bay arcades and the unbuttressed west tower with an ogival headed west lancet are 14th century. Of the 15th century are the clerestory, the roofs with bosses in the nave, aisles, and chancel, and the screen in the south aisle. One south window is probably 17th century. The church was sensitively restored by Norman Shaw in 1873. There is a vestry north of the chancel and a larger one in the NW corner. The brass to Roland Eyre, d1624, has small kneeling figures of him and his wife facing each other across prayer desks.

Hartington Church

HARTINGTON   *St Giles*   SK 130604

The church lies high above the village. The west tower of sandstone ashlar with set-back buttresses, gargoyles, battlements and pinnacles is 15th century, and so is the two storey SW porch with its west wall flush with that of the aisle. The aisled nave of three bays with quatrefoil shaped piers with fillets and the transepts and chancel are all of the period 1250-1300. There are lancets in the chancel north wall and north transept west wall. Other larger windows of the end of this period are those of five lights with intersecting tracery in the chancel east wall and the south transept end wall. The latter also has cusps and a quatrefoil at the top. Other features of this period are the south doorway, the piscinae in the transepts, and a finely moulded tomb recess in the south transept. The western aisle of the south transept with an octagonal arcade piers, and two windows in the chancel south wall are 14th century. The doorway high up in the south transept NE corner led to the former rood loft. The octagonal font with tracery panels is 15th century. Of the 13th century are several fragments of foliated cross-slabs and a half figure of a lady under a trefoiled arch.

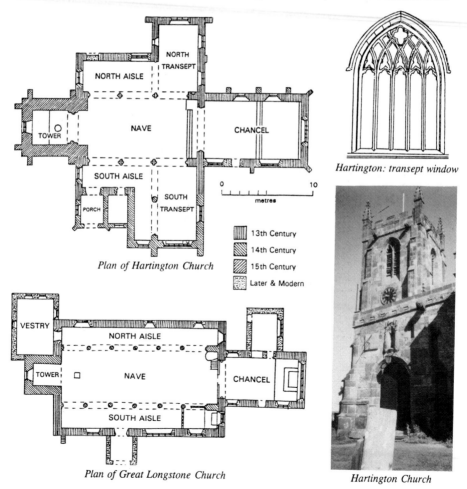

Hartington: transept window

0   10
metres

▦ 13th Century
▨ 14th Century
▧ 15th Century
▦ Later & Modern

Plan of Hartington Church

Plan of Great Longstone Church

Hartington Church

HARTSHORNE   *St Peter*   SK 327208

The nave was rebuilt in 1835 with cast-iron window tracery, but the embattled west tower and the chancel are 15th century, the font is 14th century, and there is a monument with alabaster effigies of Humphrey Dethick, d1599, and his wife.

HATHERSAGE   *St Michael*   SK 234819

The four bay arcades were mostly renewed by Butterfield in 1849-50 but that on the north with octagonal piers seems to be of c1200, whilst that on the south may correspond to building work recorded in the 1380s. The chancel may also be late 14th century. The Eyre chantry chapel on the north side of the chancel was added in 1463 and contains a tomb chest under a heavy ogee-headed recess with brasses on the lid depicting Robert Eyre, d1459 and his wife the heiress Joan Padley and their children. It was under their patronage that the church was given new embattled aisles, a south porch, a clerestory, and a diagonally buttressed west tower with a crocketed spire recessed behind battlements. Other brasses have standing figures of Ralph Eyre, d1493, and his wife, and kneeling figures of Robert Eyre, c1500, with his wife and children, and Arthur Eyre, c1560, with his wife Margaret. Members of the Ashton and Shuttleworth families are buried in a vault below the Eyre Chapel.

HAYFIELD   *St Matthew*

SK 036870

All that remains of the medieval church are bases of the piers of the arcades visible in the crypt and now supporting the present floor. The tower is of 1793 but with a clock stage added in 1894, whilst the church is of 1817-18 by Bradbury & Rangeley. The tablet to Joseph Hague, d1786, has come from the church at Glossop.

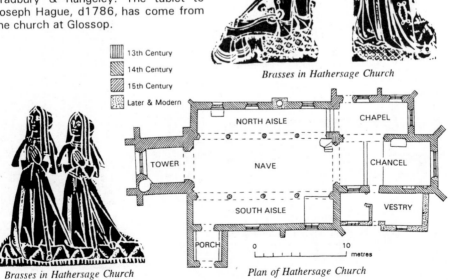

Brasses in Hathersage Church

13th Century
14th Century
15th Century
Later & Modern

Brasses in Hathersage Church

NORTH AISLE   CHAPEL

TOWER   NAVE   CHANCEL

SOUTH AISLE   VESTRY

PORCH   0   10   metres

Plan of Hathersage Church

HEAGE   *St Luke*   SK 370507

The east window of c1300 with three stepped and cusped lancets is the only relic of the medieval church. The rest of the old building (now the chancel) was rebuilt in 1646-61 with small straight-headed side windows. A taller cross-wing was added at the west end in 1826 to make a T-plan. The door lintel dated 1752 must be reset from elsewhere as there is no recognisable work of that date in the church. The polygonal bell-turret over the entrance is probably of 1896.

HEANOR   *St Lawrence*

SK 435465

The church was entirely rebuilt by Stevens & Robinson in 1866-8 except for the angle-buttressed 15th century west tower of dark grey stone.

Hathersage Church

HEATH   *All Saints*   SK 453671

In the porch of the church of 1853 by Stevens, restored in 1882-6 by Butterfield, are early medieval coffin slabs from the fragmentary old church 0.4km down the hill.

HOGNASTON   *St Bartholomew*   SK 236506

The nave south wall is partly Norman and contains a doorway with one order of colonettes with stylized beakheads and a tympanum with what appears to be a crude and disorganised representation of the Agnus Dei with figures of a bishop, a lamb and cross, two fishes, a pig, and other beasts. The 13th century west tower has lancets and clasping buttresses. The top is 15th century but the pinnacles are of the time of the rebuilding of the rest of the church in 1879-81 by F.J.Robinson. Thus the only other old parts are the arcaded Norman font and the chancel arch and a two-light window reset in the vestry which are probably both 14th century.

HOLBROOK   *St Michael*   SK 364446

The long arched windows and the pedimented porch on the north side are relics of a rebuilding in 1761. Another rebuilding in 1841 made the church into a wide rectangle with wide corner pilasters. A further remodelling in 1907-8 after a fire saw the addition of a south aisle, a chancel, and a NE porch.

Hope Church

Balguy brass, Hope

HOPE   *St Peter*   SK 173835

The 11th century cross-shaft outside the south aisle has interlace and pairs of figures. The west tower with angle-buttresses and a broach spire is early 14th century but was rebuilt in 1728. The chancel was rebuilt in 1881-2 but incorporates a piscina and sedilia of the early 14th century. The wide embattled aisles with four bay arcades on octagonal piers, and the two-storied porch and clerestory are 15th century. The windows are of three lights with panel tracery. There are large gargoyles on the south side. The south aisle east end contained a chapel of St Nicholas and a reset 13th century piscina with dogtooth lies hidden behind the organ. There are fonts of the 12th century and 1662, the latter from the lost church of Derwent now under Ladybower Reservoir. The pulpit is dated 1652 with the names of vicar Thomas Bocking and his church-wardens. There are stall backs made from former box pews dated 1587, 1632, 1658, and 1690. The paintings of Aaron and Life over the south doorway and those of Moses and Death over the north doorway are part of the 1733 scheme of "beautifying" recorded on a board in the north aisle. Near it are two 13th century foliated cross-slabs with horns to Forest officials. There is also a small brass with a crude depiction of Henry Balguy, d1685.

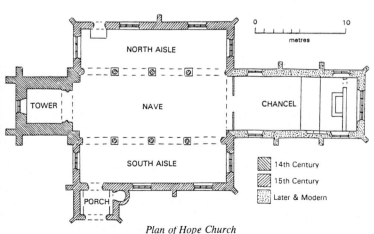

Plan of Hope Church

Horsley Church

HORSLEY   *St Clement*   SK 375445

Much of the church is early 14th century, the west tower and low broach-spire, the south doorway, the arcades with tall circular piers on the south and octagonal ones on the north, and perhaps also of that period are the sedilia with cusped ogival arches and shields in the spandrels. Most of the windows are segment headed and 15th century work, as are the font, and the clerestory and battlements throughout the church, a rededication being recorded in 1450.

ILKESTON   *St Mary*   SK 466417

The nave was doubled in length when the church was enlarged in 1909-10 and the tower rebuilt in a new position. Originally early 13th century with a spire, it was rebuilt except for the tower arch in 1723 and given a classical style top. The original south arcade of c1200 had its piers raised to match a north arcade with octagonal piers added in the early 14th century. The fine sedilia and double piscina date the chancel to the 1280s but the exterior is mostly rebuilt and the east window is entirely of 1853-5. The late 14th century north chapel contained the chantry of St Peter and has a finely moulded arcade to the chancel. The stone chancel screen with cusped ogee arches with a quatrefoil in each spandrel is early 14th century, a rare survival. The effigy of a cross-legged knight is assumed to be Sir William de Cantelupe, d1309.

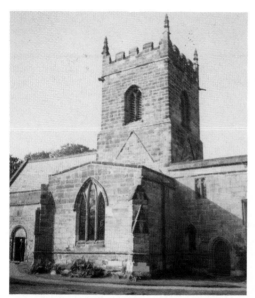

Kedleston Church

Doorway at Kedleston

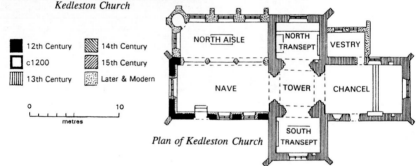

12th Century   14th Century

c1200   15th Century

13th Century   Later & Modern

0   10
metres

NORTH AISLE   NORTH TRANSEPT   VESTRY

NAVE   TOWER   CHANCEL

SOUTH TRANSEPT

Plan of Kedleston Church

KEDLESTON   *All Saints*   SK 312403

Despite having a Norman south doorway with chevrons on the arch, one order of columns with beakheads, and a defaced tympanum with beasts, the church is mostly late 13th century and has a crossing tower with transepts still retaining their original end windows of three stepped lancets. The chancel has mostly new windows although the piscina and south doorway and one small cusped lancet are original. The east end was made Classical in the late 17th century and has a pedimented sundial with vases on either side. The north aisle designed by Bodley was added in 1907-13 as a memorial to the wife of Lord Curzon, Viceroy of India. The upper parts of the tower are 15th century. In the chancel floor is a slab with the heads of a knight and lady of c1300 within quatrefoils. There is also a 13th century foliated cross slab. In a recess in the chancel south wall is an effigy of Sir John Curzon, d1446. A fine alabaster tomb chest bears effigies of Sir John Curzon, c1490, and his wife. Brasses depict Richard Curzon, d1496, and his wife, and there is an incised slab to William Curzon, d1547. The rather poor wall-monument to Sir John Curzon, 1686, was erected as early as 1664. There are other monuments to Sir John Curzon, d1727, and Sir Nathaniel Curzon, d1737, and another Sir Nathianiel, d1765, and his wife.

KILLAMARSH   *St Giles*   SK 462810

The Norman south doorway has one order of colonettes, leaf capitals and chevrons on the arch. The diagonally buttressed west tower with battlements and pinnacles is 15th century, and the south window with straight sides to all the arches is early 16th century. The north aisle and vestry were added in 1895 by J.M.Brooks.

KIRK HALLAM   *All Saints*   SK 458405

The tub-shaped font with an arcade of intersecting arches and two stones in the porch with beakheads are Norman. The church is small and without aisles. The 14th century chancel has straight-headed windows and sedilia and a piscina. The short ashlar-faced tower is 15th century. The church was restored by G.E.Street in 1859.

KIRK IRETON   *Holy Trinity*   SK 269502

The three bay south and north arcades are of c1180 and c1200 respectively. The south doorway goes with the earlier arcade, and the low tower is contemporary with the other one. The embattled 14th century chancel and contemporary vestry have a doorway between them with fleurons on the voussoirs. The embattled south chapel with an ogival arch towards the chancel is 15th century, as is the north aisle.

KIRK LANGLEY   *St Michael*   SK 286389

The sedilia and the north doorway date the chancel as early 14th century, and the windows and arcade of the north aisle are of the same period. The ashlar-faced west tower with angle buttresses connected by a horizontal band below the battlements is 15th century. The south aisle windows and the clerestory date from the restoration of 1885 by Bodley and Garner.The tower screen may be as early as c1300 and there is a parclose screen of the 15th century. There is an incised slab on a tomb-chest with twisted columns to Henry Pole, d1559, and his wife.

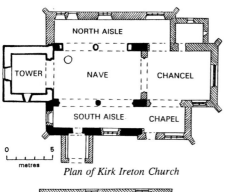

Plan of Kirk Ireton Church

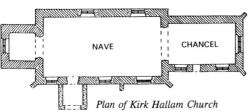

Plan of Kirk Hallam Church

Killamarsh Church

KNIVETON   *St Michael*   SK 210504

The nave is Norman with an original south doorway with a bear carved on the keystone. The small west tower with lancets and a short spire is 13th century. The chancel is 15th century. The south porch, one north window, and another in the chancel are 16th century and there are several later windows. The 13th century font has trefoiled arches and fleur-de-lis.

LITTLEOVER   *St Peter*   SK 332343

The bellcote and north aisle are of 1856, and the south aisle is of 1908, whilst the west end was enlarged by Sebastian Comper in 1959-61. The Norman doorway until then in the west wall was moved to provide access to the belfry. A wall-monument has kneeling figures of Sir Richard Harpur, d1635 and his wife facing each other.

LONG EATON   *St Laurence*   SK 492337

Much of the church dates from a rebuilding by Street in 1868 when the Norman nave became the south aisle of a new nave and the old chancel became the organ chamber serving a new chancel. The organ now lies over a new vestry of 1905. The old nave has an original window and a south doorway with one order of colonettes and arches with beakheads and chain-links. The straight-headed windows and the diagonally buttressed ashlar-faced tower and with a recessed spire west of the old nave are 14th century. There are loose fragments of another Norman doorway in the chancel.

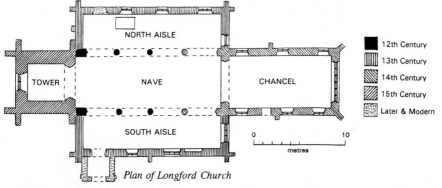

TOWER   NAVE   CHANCEL   NORTH AISLE   SOUTH AISLE

	12th Century
	13th Century
	14th Century
	15th Century
	Later & Modern

0   metres   10

Plan of Longford Church

Kniveton Church

LONGFORD   *St Chad*   SK 215383

The church lies close to the hall. Three bays of the north arcade are Norman with circular piers with multi-scalloped capitals and unchamfered two-step arches. The south arcade has Norman piers which were heightened c1300 when the aisles were rebuilt with windows of twin lancets with pierced spandrels. A fourth bay was added when a new chancel was erected in the early 14th century. Some of the seats in it have old poppy heads. The clerestory and the ashlar-faced west tower with angle buttresses and pairs of two-light bell-openings in each side are 15th century. There is a mutilated effigy in a recess in the chancel, and another recess in the south aisle contains an effigy thought to be Sir Nicholas Longford, d1357. Two other effigies on the aisle floor are thought to be his namesake grandson, d1402, and great-grandson, d1429. There are also effigies of a later Sir Nicholas, d1610, and his wife, and the later monuments to the Coke family, eventually Earls of Leicester, include a pyramid to Sir Edward Coke, d1733.

LULLINGTON   *All Saints*   SK 250130

The chancel, vestry, south aisle and the north windows are all of 1861-2, so that the only old parts are the masonry of the nave north wall and the diagonally buttressed west tower. The broach-spire with two tiers of dormer windows was rebuilt in 1776.

Long Eaton Church   *Longford Church*

MACKWORTH   *All Saints*   SK 320378

The church lies alone in a field. The ashlar-faced west tower with angle buttresses connected by a band below the battlements and a recessed spire is 15th century. The only access to the tower is by a doorway from the nave with slots for a draw-bar. The arcades look 14th century but the north aisle west window of two lights with a pierced spandrel looks earlier. The sedilia show that the chancel is also early 14th century. The aisle windows and the two storey south porch are 15th century. The lavish alabaster vestry door surround is of 1886. On a tomb chest is an effigy of Edward Mundy, d1607.

MAPPLETON   *St Mary*   SK 166480

This is an 18th century building with arched windows and a west tower bearing an octagonal dome with a lantern. The tower masonry, however, is probably medieval. The west porch has been moved from the south wall.

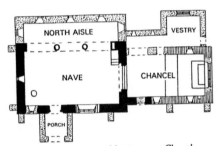

Plan of Marston Montgomery Church

■ 12th Century	▥ 16th Century
□ c1200	▦ 18th Century
▥ 13th Century	▦ Later & Modern
▨ 15th Century	

0 ─────────── 10
metres

Mackworth Church

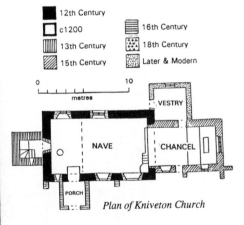

Plan of Kniveton Church

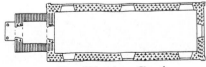

Plan of Mappleton Church

Mappleton Church

MARSTON-ON-DOVE   *St Mary*   SK 234296

The wide 13th century chancel has lancet windows and a small south doorway with one order of colonettes. The south aisle with windows with flowing tracery and a two bay arcade with a quatrefoil shaped pier is early 14th century. The ashlar faced tower with a recessed spire with three tiers of dormer windows is also 14th century and contains a bell cast in 1366. The clerestory and some features of the nave north wall are 15th century. The 18th century organ and case is from Sudbury Hall.

MARSTON MONTGOMERY   *St Giles*   SK 134378

The nave and the plain chancel arch are Norman. The nave has an original small west window and a south doorway with one order of colonettes and an incised cross. The chancel doorway and the font are also Norman. The north arcade with circular piers and single-chamfered arches is of c1200. The chancel east end has 13th century lancets and there is one nave south window with intersecting tracery. The pyramidal bellcote and the vestry and porch were added by St Aubyn in 1875-7, when the north aisle was rebuilt and several buttresses added to nave and chancel.

MATLOCK   *St Giles*   SK 301598

Only the big Norman font with crescents and ribbed angles, the 15th century west tower with diagonal buttresses, and a monument to Anthony Woolley, d1576, are old. The chancel was rebuilt in 1859, and the nave was rebuilt with very wide aisles in 1871 by Benjamin Wilson. The south chapel was added in 1898 by P.H.Currey.

MELBOURNE   *St Michael & St Mary*   SK 388250

This is one of the most ambitiously planned Norman parish churches in Britain with an aisled nave extending six bays from a twin tower west facade of the sort normally found only in cathedral and abbey churches to a crossing tower with transepts. Originally the chancel had an apse and the transepts had apsidal east chapels of which the entrance arches remain. The church was presumably begun after the living of Melbourne went to the Bishop of Carlisle when that see was founded in 1133. The arcades have piers 1.2m in diameter placed close together so that the arches are stilted to obtain enough height. The bases have angle spurs and the capitals are scalloped. Coupled wall shafts on the capitals suggest that transverse arches and perhaps vaults were intended. On the north side is a clerestory with windows which have nook-shafts on the outside, whilst inside is a wall-passage with tripartite stepped openings. The clerestory on the south side is 13th century. There are tiers of openings above the crossing arches. The chancel windows have nook-shafts both inside and out and evidence of blank arcading in a former upper storey. Each transept has a small doorway with an order of colonettes.

The west front was never fully completed, the towers rising no higher than the main roof ridge, and in any case it is visually compromised by a tithe barn placed far too close to the west. There is a central west portal with four orders of colonettes with chevrons on the arches. The towers have very broad flat buttresses. The lowest stages of the towers are groin vaulted, and so is the space between them which carries a broad arch with chevrons open to the nave, and a gallery or balcony above.

Interior of Melbourne Church

West doorway at Melbourne

Melbourne Church

Later alterations are surprisingly few, just 15th century windows in the aisles and in the straight wall replacing the original main apse, and a tall upper stage of the central tower added in 1602. The chancel has a 16th century roof. The western crossing piers have 14th century wall paintings including a large horned devil with outspread wings, two women each with a smaller devil on her back, and traces of a Passion series including the Flagellation and Crucifixion. The Norman font has a bowl on four squat columns. Gathered together in a vestry formed in the south transept are a 13th century foliated cross-slab, a damaged early 14th century effigy of a knight under a 15th century arched recess, and three alabaster slabs to Henry Hardie, d1613, Anne Harding, d1673, and Sir Robert Harding, d1679.

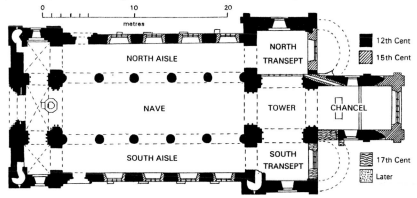

Plan of Melbourne Church

MICKLEOVER   *All Saints*   SK 305342

The church was once dedicated to St Nicholas. The chancel has 14th century windows with intersecting tracery, a priest's doorway with a round head and roll-moulding, a piscina, and a built-in bible rest. The low west tower with angle buttresses, the south aisle and the octagonal font may also be 14th century. In 1858-9 H.I.Stevens rebuilt the north arcade and the chancel arch and extended the north aisle. G.I.Larkin added the vestry and north aisle chapel in 1965-7.

MONYASH   *St Leonard*   SK 151665

The church is said to have been founded c1198 and much of it is of the half century or so after then. It then comprised a west tower with lancets, a nave and transepts and a chancel which retains more lancets and segmental arched sedilia and piscina decorated with dogtooth. The chancel arch has head corbels with stiff-leaf capitals. The tower stair is unusual in that it starts from the south aisle. The south transept has straight-headed windows likely to be of c1348 when a chantry chapel was founded in it, whilst the north transept was rebuilt by Butterfield as part of his general restoration of 1884-7, when the outside of the chancel was refaced. The south porch and many of the furnishings are also his. There are further late 14th century square-headed windows in the aisles and the three bay arcades are probably also of that period. The 15th century font has an octagonal bowl on a quatrefoil stem carved with animals. The large chest may be 13th century.

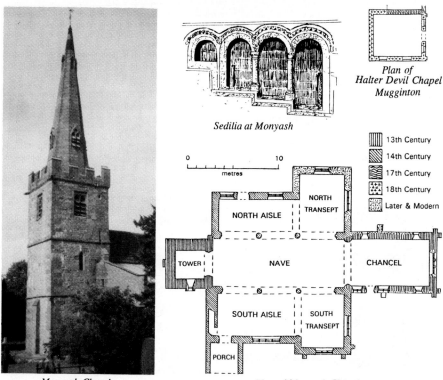

Sedilia at Monyash

Plan of
Halter Devil Chapel
Mugginton

13th Century
14th Century
17th Century
18th Century
Later & Modern

Monyash Church

Plan of Monyash Church

MORLEY *St Matthew* SK 396409

The Norman two bay south arcade has a circular pier with a scalloped capital and unmoulded arches, the east respond capital having sparse leaf forms. The north arcade is early 13th century. Of the early 14th century are the south porch and the chancel, although the east window has been renewed. According to inscriptions on brasses the north chapel with a four-centred arch and many original floor tiles was added by Ralph de Stathum, d1380, and the west tower with a round SW stair turret and angle buttresses with many set-offs was added by Ralph's widow Goditha and her son who died in 1403. The south chapel was added by John Stathum, d1453, although the brasses of him and his wife with St Christopher above lie in the north chapel. The clerestory is also 15th century, whilst the straight-headed aisle windows are late 14th century. In the north chapel there is much fine stained glass originally made for the cloister of Dale Abbey in the 1480s and brought here in the 1540s. Scenes include the legend of St Robert of Knaresborough and the Invention of the Holy Cross. There is also much Victorian glass.

On a tomb chest in the south aisle are brasses of Thomas Strathum, d1470, with two wives and scrolls leading up to figures of St Christopher, St Anne, and the Virgin and Child. Under an arch between the chancel and south chapel is a tomb chest with brasses of Henry Stathum, d1480, and three wives and children. In the chapel itself are brasses of John Sacheverell, killed at the battle of Bosworth in 1485, and his wife and children. A tomb chest between the chancel and north chapel has a tomb chest with brasses of Henry Sacheverell, d1558, and his wife. The finest of all the monuments is a recumbent effigy of Katherine Babington, d1543. In the north chapel floor are four incised slabs to Sacheverell children who died in 1625, 1626, 1638, and 1639. There are also alabaster effigies of Jacynth Sacheverell, d1656, and his wife, and frontal half-figures in the south chapel of Jonathan Sacheverell, d1662 and his wife. The monuments to Henry Sacheverell, d1662, William, d1691, and Robert, d1714, are without effigies, but the first two have tomb chests.

MORTON *Holy Cross* SK 407602

Only the 15th century west tower with diagonal buttresses and eight pinnacles on the battlements, plus the late 13th century north arcade with circular piers survived the rebuilding of the church by T.C.Hine in 1850.

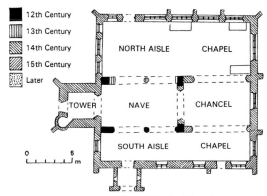

Plan of Morley Church

Morley Church

Mugginton Church

MUGGINTON   *All Saints*   SK 284429

The Norman west tower has a later central buttress half concealing its former west doorway. Other original features are the window high up facing the nave, the bell-opening on the north side and the corbel-table. The tower arch with keeled half-round responds and a plain unchamfered arch is perhaps slightly later, and the top stage is later still. The south aisle west window and south doorway are probably 18th century, whilst the arcade is probably early 14th century. The south chapel, the roofs, the screen with panel tracery, and hexagonal font with pointed quatrefoils are 15th century. The font has, however, been recut later. The pews are dated by an inscription to 1600. A section of box-pews are later. On a tomb chest are fine and large brasses of Nicholas Kniveton, d1400, and his wife.

Some 2.5km to the north is Halter Devil Chapel, built by Francis Brown in 1723 adjacent to his farmhouse, and enlarged in 1890. One dark night Brown swore he would ride into Derby then and there even if he had to halter the Devil. He then discovered that his horse had horns, i.e. had indeed been taken over by the Devil.

NETHERSEAL   *St Peter*   SK 288129

The church was mostly rebuilt in 1877 by Blomfield but the wide north aisle with a four bay arcade is 13th century, the diagonally buttressed west tower is 15th century, and the chancel has some old work in the priest's doorway and an incised slab to rector Roger Douton, d1500, under an arch on the north side.

NEWBOLD   *No dedication known*   SK 370734

This plain rectangular building with a defaced Norman tympanum over the doorway, late medieval style windows, and a roof with bosses on the tie-beams, was sacked by a Protestant mob after James II granted it for use by Roman Catholics. The pediment-like gable with pinnacles may be a repair following this incident.

Halter Devil Chapel, near Mugginton

NEWTON SOLNEY   *St Mary*   SK 279258

Of the Norman period are a plain north doorway and fragments of a more ambitious doorway, presumably once set on the south side, but now built into the north wall of the 14th century tower with a recessed spire. The arcades are 14th century, too, but the north aisle must be earlier, with single lancets at either end and coupled ones facing north. Inside these have heads at the springer between the two openings. The straight-headed chancel windows and the clerestory are 15th century. There is an alabaster effigy of a knight of c1375, plus two earlier effigies of knights, one headless (probably Sir Alured de Sulney, c1250) and the other cross-legged and now very damaged. The monument with a semi-reclining figure of Sir Henry Every, d1709, carved by Thomas Carter, was erected c1734.

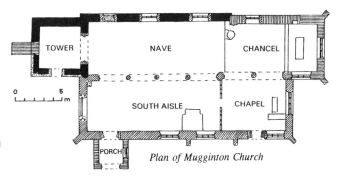

Brass at Mugginton

Plan of Mugginton Church

NORBURY   *St Mary and St Barlok*   SK 126424

The chancel dwarfs the rest of the church and is a splendid piece with a five-light east window and three-light south windows with cusped intersecting tracery filling the whole space available between the bold buttresses. These windows have original glass with coats of arms. The inclusion of the arms of Bruce, who was at war with England from 1306 onwards, make a date immediately before that year likely. The chancel must have been built at the expense of Sir Henry Fitzherbert, d1315, whose effigy lay in the middle of it until it was transferred to the SE chapel in 1892. The glass in the east window is 15th century work moved from the nave and aisle. Shafts running up between the embrasures on the chancel side-walls hint that a vault may have been intended. In the late 15th century the chancel was given a new roof of flatter profile and unusual saw-teeth type crenellations. There is no chancel arch.

The nave including perhaps its clerestory, and the unusual porch-tower in the middle of its south side were built by Nicholas Fitzherbert, d1473. His tomb and effigy now lie in the chancel, but originally lay in the chapel east of the tower, where his arms appear in the east window. His wives Alice Bothe (heiress of Norbury) and Isabel Ludlow appear on the west end of the tomb chest. A similar tomb probably made at the same time (c1500-10) bears effigies of Ralph Fitzherbert, d1483, and his wife the heiress Elizabeth Marshall, d1491. This tomb formerly lay where the organ now stands at the east end of the north aisle. The aisle has a four bay arcade and was probably built by this couple, unless it is as early as the time of Nicholas. Ralph's will, incidentally, refers to the dedication, very rare, of the church to St Barlok, an Irish abbot and bishop. The chapel west of the tower is thought to have been built by John Fitzherbert, d1531, author of books on husbandry and surveying. His plain tomb in the chapel was moved under its entrance arch in 1892 to make space for the chapel to be adapted as a vestry.

The other monuments include incised slabs to rector Henry Prince, d1500, with a chalice, and Alice, c1460, and Elizabeth, d1491, respective wives of Nicholas and Ralph Fitzherbert. Elizabeth is depicted in a burial shroud. There are brasses to Sir Anthony Fitzherbert, d1538, and his wife Maud and their daughters. The brass was made before Maud died in 1551, her year of death being left blank on the inscription. On the reverse of these plates are older engravings, the two main figures having been cut from a large figure of c1316 to Matilda de Verdun, probably plundered from the dissolved abbey of Croxden, whilst other parts are engraved on mid 15th century plates taken from Calwich Abbey. Ann, d1653, wife of William Fitzherbert, who has a stone in the chancel, was the last of the family buried at Norbury. Other features of interest are the 13th century font with a bowl on clustered shafts, the much restored screen, the chancel seats with poppy-heads and tracery with Flamboyant

motifs, and fragments of two 11th century cross-shafts with interlace and one small figure, these having been discovered during restoration work in 1899.

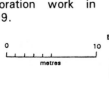

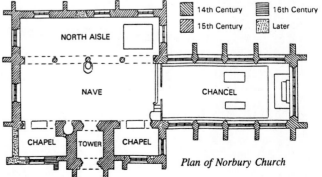

Plan of Norbury Church

Norbury Church

Tomb recess, North Wingfield

NORMANTON-BY-DERBY

St Giles　SK 350336

The church was rebuilt in 1861 by Giles & Brookhouse and given a new east window in 1882, but in the porch is a Norman carved stone from a lintel of the old church.

NORTH WINGFIELD　*St Lawrence*　SK 405645

The church was once dedicated to St Helen. The Norman north transept has an original east window. The eastern bays of the north arcade are 13th century, whilst the chancel is 14th century with a contemporary north vestry and an east window with reticulated tracery and later medieval glass. The nave roof with old tie-beams and broad trefoil tracery above is thought to be 14th century. In the 15th century the north arcade was lengthened by two bays (with upside down shields on the pier capitals) to connect up with a high new tower with angle buttresses and pairs of two-light bell-openings. The body of the church was then embattled and a porch was added with a pointed tunnel-vault with transverse arches. The south aisle was rebuilt in 1860, the north aisle was heavily restored in 1872 when the existing clerestory windows were provided, and there was a general restoration in 1879. The font is of 1662. There is a defaced 15th century relief of the Martyrdom of St Lawrence under a cusped ogival arch in the south aisle. The many mutilated monuments include foliated cross-slabs and an effigy of a priest of c1300 in the porch and two effigies of Deincourt knights under ogival-headed recesses inside and outside the chancel.

OCKBROOK   *All Saints*   SK 424357

The only ancient surviving parts are the font with interlaced arches and the west tower, which are Norman, the latter having a 13th century broach spire and a big later NE buttress, plus the chest of 1662, and an early 16th century screen from the Wigston Hospital at Leicester. The top part was removed in 1967 and made into a communion rail. The chancel was rebuilt by Thomas Pares in 1803 and a burial vault then added on the north side with a family pew above, now replaced by the organ. The nave was widened to the north in 1814-15 and to the south in 1835.

PARWICH   *St Peter*   SK near Tissington

The church was rebuilt in 1873-4 by Stevens and Robinson but in the tower are the original Norman chancel arch and north doorway, the latter with a tympanum depicting the Agnus Dei with a lamb and cross and a stag each standing on a serpent, above which are a bird, a pig and a lion.

PENTRICH   *St Matthew*   SK 391526

The church was once dedicated to St Helen. The lower stage of the west tower and the five bay arcades with single chamfered round arches on circular piers are of c1200. The tower buttresses and embattled top, the south porch, the nave clerestory and battlements, the narrow south aisle and the widened north aisle are of c1380-1400, whilst the chancel with a five-light east window is 15th century. The clerestory window lintels are old tomb slabs reused. The font is dated 1662 on the base but the bowl with low arches in relief may be Norman. There is a Rococo style wall-monument to Edmund Horn, d1764.

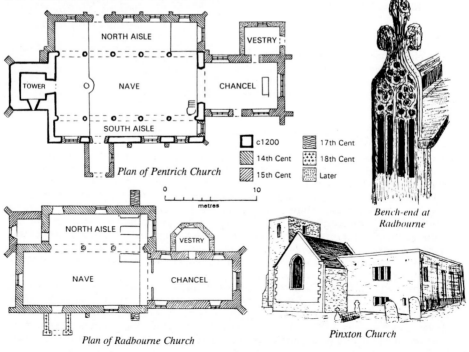

Plan of Pentrich Church

c1200 14th Cent 15th Cent 17th Cent 18th Cent Later

0 10
metres

Bench-end at Radbourne

Plan of Radbourne Church

Pinxton Church

Pentrich Church

PINXTON   *St Helen*   SK 454550

Of the medieval church dedicated to St John the Evangelist there remain only the 13th century west tower and a short section of the nave north wall with one lancet. The tower has a 14th century window on the south side. In 1750 a large new church with arched windows and a plain Venetian east window was built at right angles to the old nave. An aisle and porch were added to this new church in 1939.

PLEASLEY   *St Michael*   SK 505646

The church is mostly 13th century with a long unaisled nave. Earlier are the Norman font with a seated figure probably of the Virgin, and the chancel arch with a double billet frieze on the label and two roll-mouldings in the arch. The font bowl of 1662 is set on an upturned 11th or 12th century base,

QUARNDON   *St Paul*   SK 335410

A little way to the south of the church of 1874 by Giles & Brookhouse was an ivy-covered fragment of the walling of the tower of the old church.

RADBOURNE   *St Andrew*   SK 285360

The church lies in the grounds of the hall. The nave with one south window with cusped intersected tracery, and the north aisle with a three bay arcade with hexagonal piers are of c1300-30. The sedilia dates the chancel to the early 13th century. The ashlar faced 15th century tower with diagonal buttresses has an unusual position in the NW corner. There are late medieval bench and bench ends with poppy-heads from Dale Abbey, and the west pew has a front of 16th century linenfold panelling with a motif of grapes and vines. There are incised slabs to Peter de la Pole, d1432, and Ralph de la Pole, d1455, depicted with their wives, and there is a 13th century foliated cross slab. An alabaster tomb chest bears effigies of John de la Pole, d1491, and his wife. The wall-monument by Grinling Gibbons to German Pole, with a big sarcophagus in relief surmounted by an urn, was erected in 1683.

REPTON *St Wystan* SK 303272

Repton was the capital of South Mercia under King Peada, who induced his people to adopt Christianity. A double monastery for men and women was founded here in the late 7th century. Within the church the kings Aethelbald and Wiglaf were buried here in 757 and 840. St Wystan was buried in his grandfather Wiglaf's mausoleum after being murdered in 849. His body was an object of veneration until removed by King Cnut (1016-35) to Evesham. The Danes probably destroyed the abbey when they wintered at Repton in 874. An Augustinian priory was founded close to the church in 1172 and fragments of it remain in the buildings of the famous school.

It thus comes as no surprise that the church has major Saxon remains. What is now the sanctuary was the east arm of a church which was cruciform, probably with a tower over the wide central body of which the eastern corners remain. Parts also survive of the east and north walls of the original north transept or porticus. The sanctuary has thin pilaster strips running from a string-course to end in splayed capitals below the eaves. Stairs in the transepts lead down to the crypt, a chamber 5m square divided by four central columns into nine almost square bays covered by domical vaults carried on cross-ribs. The columns are decorated with spiral fillets. There are shallow recesses, perhaps to house coffins. The dating of the Saxon parts has been debated at length. Dr H.M.Taylor, who conducted excavations in and around the church in the 1970s, considers that the crypt was originally built c760 as the burial chamber of Wiglaf with access then from the east, and that the vaults and superstructure were built c840, whilst the two stairs presently used were made to ease access for pilgrims visiting St Wystan's tomb c850.

Repton Church

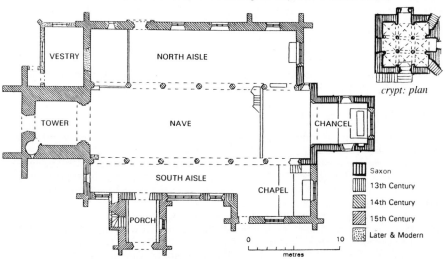

crypt: plan

VESTRY

NORTH AISLE

TOWER

NAVE

CHANCEL

SOUTH AISLE

CHAPEL

PORCH

	Saxon
	13th Century
	14th Century
	15th Century
	Later & Modern

0   10
metres

Plan of Repton Church

By the 13th century the present nave continuing the Saxon central body to the west had been laid out and provided with a south aisle. By 1340 a chapel with an unusual south window had been built on the side of the south porticus and a wide new north aisle had been erected, whilst new arcades of six bays with hexagonal piers were laid out to connect the Saxon parts with a west tower with bold angle buttresses and a spire 63m high. The chancel east window is also of that period, while the chancel side windows are 13th century lancets. The clerestory, roof and battlements of the nave, plus the large two storey south porch are 15th century. There are no ancient furnishings but the monuments include an alabaster effigy of a knight of c1400, an incised alabaster slab to Gilbert Thacker, d1563, and his wife, and a tablet with a frontal bust of Francis Thacker, d1710.

RISLEY   *All Saints*   SK 461357

Michael Willoughby built this chapel in 1593, the date that appears over the south doorway, although it was not consecrated until 1632. The doorway has a four-centred arch with a hood-mould. The south windows are round headed with intersecting tracery. The west tower has bell-openings with two lancets under an round arch. The alabaster font with strapwork decoration and the screen with cherubim on the cross beam are of about the same period as the church.

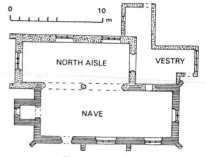

Plan of Risley Church

Risley Church

ROSLISTON   *St Mary*   SK 244168

A tiny 14th century west tower with a broach spire rises from a massive base. The wide main body of the church is of 1819. At the east end are three small chambers with the middle one containing altars. The others have doorways to the outside.

ROWSLEY   *St Katherine*   SK 255661

The church was rebuilt in 1855 by Salvin junior, and was given a north aisle in 1859. The Saxon cross-head with curling ends is thought to be mid 9th century.

SANDIACRE   *St Giles*   SK 480373

The large Norman nave has two big original windows high up with nook-shafts inside and out (both later lengthened downwards) and a south doorway of three orders with roll-mouldings and capitals with volutes and scallops. The chancel arch is also Norman and has an imp on the south capital. The tall and long chancel is thought to date from the 1340s, when Bishop Norbury of Lichfield held the prebend of Sandiacre. There are big crocketed pinnacles on the buttresses and a quatrefoil frieze above the tall windows of three lights, whilst the east window is of six lights. The tracery includes patterns of stars and leaf shapes. On the north side are fragments of the original glass. There are fine triple sedilia and a piscina with crocketed canopies. Of the same period are the four light window in the nave south wall and the font. The low west tower with a spire with small broaches is 13th century. The clerestory is the only 15th century contribution to this interesting building.

Sandiacre Church

Rosliston Church

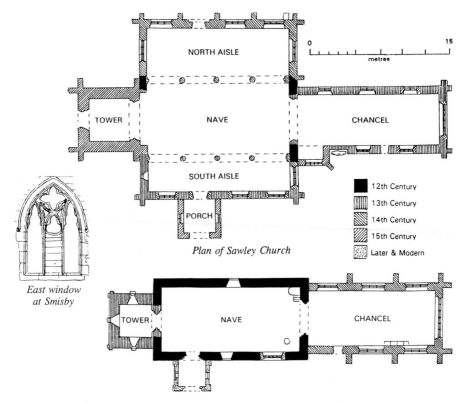

NORTH AISLE

TOWER   NAVE   CHANCEL

SOUTH AISLE

PORCH

Plan of Sawley Church

0   15
metres

■ 12th Century
▥ 13th Century
▨ 14th Century
▧ 15th Century
▦ Later & Modern

*East window
at Smisby*

TOWER   NAVE   CHANCEL

Plan of Sandiacre Church

SAWLEY   *All Saints*   SK 472313

Towards the wide nave there is a lot of bare wall above the Norman chancel arch. The 13th century chancel has windows of paired lancets with a pierced spandrel, but the tracery of the five light east window appears to be Victorian. The arcades are of the same period or slightly later and there is a small west lancet in the south aisle, whilst the other windows have mid 14th century recticulated tracery. Of the 15th century are the clerestory and the battlements upon it and the aisle outer wall, the chancel screen and parts of two other screens, and the west tower with angle buttresses and a spire recessed behind the battlements. The screen dividing off the chancel east end to form a vestry is medieval and on the south side is a bay window with panelled sides and a four-centred vault which formed a chantry chapel containing the effigy of John Bothe, Treasurer of Lichfield Cathedral. A tomb chest under a recess in the chancel north wall bears small brasses of Roger Bothe, d1467, and his wife. There are larger brasses of Robert Bothe, d1478, and his wife on a tomb chest under the chancel arch. In the north aisle east end are brasses of Richard Shylton, d1510, and his wife. Next to them is an effigy of a priest brought in from a recess outside. There are also fragments of another important monument which was dismantled in the 1830s. The pulpit and tester are of 1636. The roof and stalls contain some original late medieval work.

Sawley Church

SCARCLIFFE   *St Leonard*   SK 496687

The church was once dedicated to St Giles. The Norman south doorway has an order of colonettes and a roll-moulding in the arch, the lintel being decorated with stars, wheels, and saltire crosses. The chancel doorway is Norman too, but renewed. There are 13th century lancets in the chancel side walls, but the tower of that period was rebuilt in 1842. The nave south side is embattled and has late 16th or 17th century windows. Others on the north are smaller. The chest is late medieval and the font cover is of 1686. The fine 13th century female effigy holding a child is probably of Constantia de Frecheville, d1175.

SCROPTON   *St Paul*   SK 192302

The church was rebuilt by Ferrey in 1855-6 but it contains an incised slab to William Schower, d1495, and an alabaster tomb of Nicholas Agard, d1515 and his wives Margery Vernon and Isabel Ferrers.

SHIRLAND   *St Leonard*   SK 400586

The church is mostly 15th century work. It has a diagonally buttressed west tower with eight pinnacles on the battlements. The aisles are embattled and so is the clerestory, in this case with pinnacles. The south porch is vaulted with a pointed transverse arch. The painting of the Crucifixion and St Mary Magdalen is probably North Italian work of the mid 15th century. An effigy thought to have been of Henry, 5th Lord Grey of Wilton, d1396, has vanished from the tomb chest in a large ogee-headed recess in the chancel north wall, but shields remain with the Grey arms. Only one panel remains of another tomb chest. An incised slab of John Revell, d1537, and his wife lies on a tomb chest with large cusped quatrefoils in the north aisle. There is a wall monument to John Revell, d1699, and his son William, d1706.

SHIRLEY   *St Michael*   SK 219417

The chancel and the south aisle with an arcade of octagonal piers are 14th century, although the main east window is later, and the south windows are Victorian. The north aisle is of 1842 but upon the outside east wall is a worn stone carved with beast and birds from a Norman lintel. The west gallery on cast-iron columns and the box pews must also be of 1842, whilst the west tower is of 1861. There is a late medieval incised slab of a priest.

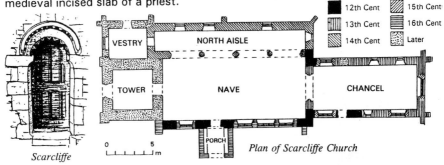

Scarcliffe

Plan of Scarcliffe Church

Scarcliffe Church

SMISBY   *St James*   SK 347191

The low south arcade of three bays with circular piers is 13th century, whilst the chancel and perhaps also the west tower are 14th century. There are many post-Reformation plain mullioned windows, and one in the aisle east wall with a transom as well. The 16th century linenfold panelling at the east end is from Ashby-de-la-Zouch Castle. The monuments include a fine mid 14th century effigy of Joan Comyn of Smisby, an incised alabaster slab to William Kendall, d1500, and his wife, and a wall monument with large kneeling figures of Henry Kendal, d1627, and his wife.

SNELSTON   *St Peter*   SK 155434

The nave and chancel were rebuilt in 1825 and again in 1907 by Hodgson Fowler, so only the diagonally buttressed NW tower with battlements and pinnacles is old.

SOMERSAL HERBERT   *St Peter*   SK 136352

The church was dedicated to St Blaise in the 16th century. The present building is mostly of 1874 by C.J.Neale, with a west tower added in 1912, but it contains a Norman font with intersecting arches with lozenges and circles above, and the brick porch with rusticated stone quoins must be 18th century.

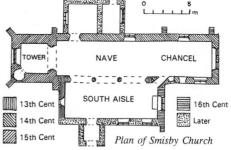

Plan of Smisby Church

Porch, Somersal Herbert

Snelston Church

South Wingfield Church

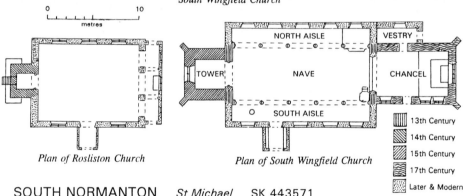

Plan of Rosliston Church   *Plan of South Wingfield Church*

13th Century
14th Century
15th Century
17th Century
Later & Modern

SOUTH NORMANTON   *St Michael*   SK 443571

The oldest part is the reset head of the door to the north vestry which is of c1250-75, being pointed and trefoiled with dogtooth and cusps like stiff-leaf fleur-de-lis. The octagonal font is probably 14th century. The west tower with diagonal buttresses is 15th century and the north aisle with a three bay arcade on thin piers is likely to be 16th century. The south aisle is of 1878. There is a wall monument with two standing putti to Robert Revel, d1714.

SOUTH WINGFIELD   *All Saints*   SK 384558

The church lies alone by the Amber, away from both the village and the ruined manor house. The nave and narrow aisles with arcades of five bays with circular piers with occasional nailhead decoration and one keeled respond are 13th century. The arched and unmoulded windows are of 1803. The chancel is Jacobean but with the features renewed in 1877. The diagonally buttressed west tower is 15th century. The large tub-shaped font is Norman.

Stanton-by-Dale Church   *Spondon Church*

SPONDON   *St Werburgh*   SK 375380

Despite restorations in 1826 and 1891-2, the latter by J.Oldrid Scott, this is essentially a complete church of the decade after 1340 when the old church was destroyed by fire and the villagers were exempted from taxation whilst rebuilding proceeded. It consists of a west tower with a spire recessed behind an embattled parapet, a spacious aisled nave with three bay arcades on octagonal piers, and a chancel with a low tomb recess (or Easter Sepulchre) and a built-in bible rest on the north side, and sedilia and piscina on the south. The south aisle has windows with flowing tracery whilst those in the chancel and north aisle have reticulated tracery.

STANLEY   *St Andrew*   SK 419404

Much of the church is of 1874 by Evans & Jolly, but the chancel has a large 13th century east window of three stepped lancet lights, and the nave has a small Norman south doorway with a small 13th century lancet to the east of it.

STANTON-BY-BRIDGE   *St Michael*   SK 367272

The SE corner of the nave has Saxon long-and-short work. Norman are the west window, the chancel arch and the south doorway with chevrons on the arch and one order of colonettes. The north aisle with a low three bay arcade with octagonal piers, and the chancel with bar tracery with a circled quatrefoil, are late 13th century. An effigy of a priest of c1400 lies in a recess. There are incised slabs to Richard Francis, d1530, (much damaged) and William Sacheverell, d1558. A separate slab with kneeling children is from the front of William's tomb chest.

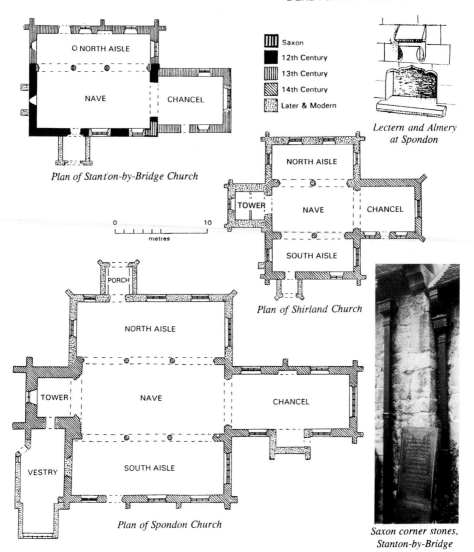

Saxon
12th Century
13th Century
14th Century
Later & Modern

O NORTH AISLE

NAVE | CHANCEL

Plan of Stanton-by-Bridge Church

0 ——— 10
metres

NORTH AISLE

TOWER | NAVE | CHANCEL

SOUTH AISLE

Plan of Shirland Church

Lectern and Almery
at Spondon

PORCH

NORTH AISLE

TOWER | NAVE | CHANCEL

VESTRY | SOUTH AISLE

Plan of Spondon Church

Saxon corner stones,
Stanton-by-Bridge

STANTON-BY-DALE   *St Michael*   SK 465382

The south doorway tympanum with a cross may be Norman. Of c1300 are the north
aisle with its windows and three bay arcade and the chancel with windows of three
stepped lancet lights. The west tower with crocketed pinnacles on the battlements
is later, and the tunnel-vaulted porch with thick transverse arches is 15th century.

STANTON-IN-THE-PEAK   *Holy Trinity*   SK 242643

Stanton was a chapel-of-ease to Youlgreave until 1838. Inside the church built in
1839 are two items given by the Thornhill family, an Italian bronze stoup dated 1596,
and a tabernacle in the Florentine Quattrocento style.

Staveley Church

STAVELEY   *St John the Baptist*   SK 434749

The original dedication was to St Mary, St John the Baptist being the dedication of another chapel in the parish which has now vanished. The font is perhaps assembled from Norman fragments. The partly renewed south doorway and the west tower with a west doorway and lancet above are 13th century. The tower arch has keeled half-round responds. The bell-stage is 15th century and the battlements and pinnacles are of 1681. The south aisle and its arcade are 15th century, whilst the north aisle is of 1865-9 by Sir G.G.Scott, although it contains a reset late medieval recess with figures and an ogee-head. There are also fragments of 14th century glass in the aisle windows. The Frecheville Chapel of the 1660s on the south side of the chancel has fine heraldic stained glass by Henry Gyles dated 1676, and contains a wall-monument with a semi-reclining effigy of Christiana Frecheville died 1653 in childbed, plus that of John, Lord Frecheville, Governor of York, d1682. Other Frecheville monuments in the chancel are the incised alabaster slab to John, d1510, and the brasses of Peter, c1480, on a tomb chest, and Piers, d1503, and his wife, set in a recess.

STEETLEY   *St Mary*   SK 544788

This is a particularly fine mid 12th century building comprising a nave, a slightly narrower and lower chancel, and a still narrower and lower east apse with a square bay west of it, the division between round and square being marked by a transverse arch of complex profile with roll mouldings. The apse is vaulted with two ribs running to meet the transverse arch, buttresses marking the position of these outside. The apse has three nook-shafted windows set on an ornamental band. There are fine arches with between the three parts, which each have corbel-tables. There are chevrons on the arch between the nave and chancel and the piers of the north respond have a double-bodied lion, and St George with a winged dragon trampling a prostrate lady. The nave and chancel lay in ruins for at least a century prior to a restoration by J.L.Pearson in 1876, and two of the four orders of colonettes of the spectacular south doorway and the gable above it are his. Original are the modest north doorway, two small west windows, and one on the south side. The chancel has a renewed south window of 14th century type. By the porch lies a Norman stone to a priest with a chalice and paten resting on an altar and a hand raised in blessing.

Steetley Chapel

Plan of Steetley Chapel

Doorway, Steetley Chapel

STONEY MIDDLETON   *St Martin*

SK 232755

In 1759 a new octagonal church with an ambulatory and a lantern storey on piers was added to the low late medieval west tower of the old church. There a circular windows in the ambulatory and semi-circular ones divided in three in the lantern. The chancel has a tall arched window with two mullions and a transom.

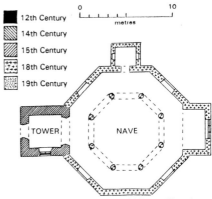

Plan of Stoney Middleton Church

Stoney Middleton Church

Brass at Tideswell

SUDBURY   *All Saints*   SK 157322

The south doorway and a small window in the Vernon Chapel are Norman but renewed. The low tower with diagonal buttresses may be of about that period but the top has a 17th century balustrade with short pinnacles. The clerestory is genuine 15th century work, but other windows in that style are of the time of Devey's restoration of 1874-5. He renewed the arcades of three bays with circular piers on the north and octagonal ones on the south plus the arch between the chancel and chapel. The defaced effigies of two women holding hearts are of c1300. The monument to John Vernon, d1600, and his wife Mary has her effigy on a tomb chest whilst his lies under a shallow arch behind and above her. Other Vernon monuments include those of Margaret, d1675, and George, d1702, and wife Catherine d1710.

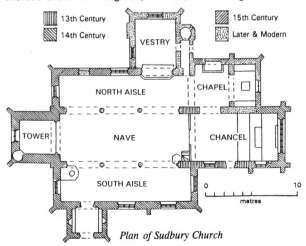

Plan of Sudbury Church

Angel stone at Sudbury

Sudbury Church

SUTTON-ON-THE-HILL   *St Michael*   SK 237343

The 14th century tower and spire were rebuilt in 1841. The rest was rebuilt in 1863 except for part of the chancel and a 14th century arcade with octagonal piers and double-chamfered arches. There are heads and leaf motifs on the label-stops. The monument to Judith Sleigh, d1634, has a black stone coffin complete with handles.

SUTTON SCARSDALE   *St Mary*   SK 443689

The church is picturesquely situated by the ruined hall. Much of it is 14th century, including several windows, the south porch, and the arcade of the north aisle and chancel chapel, whilst the diagonally buttressed west tower is 15th century. The communion rail is 17th century. The monuments include an incised slab to John Foljambe, d1499, and a wall-monument with a bust of Samuel Pierrepont, d1707.

SWARKESTON   *St James*   SK 372287

The church was mostly rebuilt by F.J.Robinson in 1874-6 except for the SW tower and the Harpur chapel on the south side of the chancel. The font is Norman and stones of that period are built into the aisle east wall. In the chapel are alabaster tomb chests with effigies of Richard Harpur, d1573, and his wife, and Sir John Harpur, d1627, and his wife, the helmet of c1580 being decorated for his funeral. In the chancel is a tomb chest with effigies of John Rolleston, d1482, and his wife.

Monument in Thorpe Church

TADDINGTON   *St Michael*   SK 142712

The west tower with a broach spire and an arch to the nave double chamfered without capitals is early 14th century. Of later in that century are the nave and aisles with lofty arcades of four bays with octagonal piers and head-corbels forming the east responds, and the fine chancel with a built-in lectern and tall straight-headed side windows and a large east window with flowing tracery. The aisles have similar windows on a more modest scale. The church was restored in 1891 by Naylor & Sale. There is a brass to Richard Blackwall, d1505, and his wife and children. The cross-shaft in the churchyard with saltire crosses and chevrons may be Norman.

TAXAL   *St James*   SK 006799

The church was originally dedicated to St Leonard. It has a 16th century west tower with 17th century pinnacles on top. The wide nave, originally with galleries, dates from a rebuilding of 1825. It was restored in 1889 when a larger new chancel was added with an organ-recess on the south and a vestry on the north. The vestry has an east extension of 1922. Inside are early 18th century altar rails with turned balusters and a tablet to Michael Heathcote, d1768, described as "Gentleman of the Pantry and Yeoman of the Mouth to his late Majesty King George III".

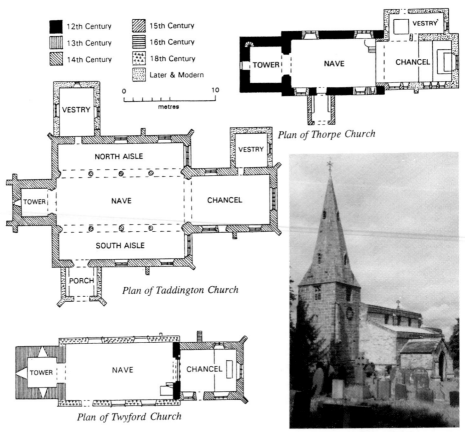

12th Century	15th Century
13th Century	16th Century
14th Century	18th Century
	Later & Modern

0 ___ metres ___ 10

Plan of Thorpe Church

Plan of Taddington Church

Plan of Twyford Church

Taddington Church

THORPE   *St Leonard*   SK 156502

The short Norman west tower has large quoins, two-light bell-openings, a corbel table and later battlements. Also Norman are the plain font and the nave with an original south doorway and window, next to which is a small 13th century window. The porch is 15th century and two north windows are 16th or 17th century. The chancel has a 15th century south window but is mostly rebuilt with a north vestry added. There is a monument to John Millward, d1632. A sundial outside is of 1767.

TIBSHELF   *St John the Baptist*   SK 441609

Only the 15th century west tower with diagonal buttresses survived the rebuilding of 1887-8 by Bodley & Garner.

TICKNALL   *St George*   SK 351241

In the church of 1842 by Stevens lie an effigy of a civilian holding a heart and an incised slab to the knight John Frances, c1375. These have come from the old church further south, of which fragments of the west tower and east end with a window with intersected tracery still stand.

TIDESWELL   *St John the Baptist*   SK 152758

This large and proud embattled 14th century church is commonly referred to as the "Cathedral of the Peak". The wide nave of c1320-40, still retaining its original roof, has arcades of four bays opening into aisles and much wider east arches opening into transepts. The arcades have piers of a quatrefoil section with sunk hollow between the lobes. The aisles and transept side walls have three light windows, whilst those in the transept end walls are huge and of five lights, flowing tracery being used throughout. At the SW corner is a rib-vaulted porch with an upper room reached by a tiny stair in the porch SW corner. The west tower of c1370-1400 is very lofty and has angle buttresses. The tower arch and the five light west window of Perpendicular type are very lofty. At the top the tower has four octagonal corner turrets surmounted by thick pinnacles. There are roof marks and a chancel arch of an intended smaller chancel which may or may not have actually been built. The present chancel, wider than the nave, was erected at the expense of John Foljambe, d1383, during the last twenty years of his life. It has a five-light east window still with flowing tracery and three-light side windows in each of the four bays. The dividing buttresses have pinnacles and there are ogee-headed sedilia. A vestry is created by an original wall dividing off half of the east bay, the wall having niches with tall canopies for statues. The octagonal font with shields and panels is late 14th or 15th century. In the north transept are old seats, two of which have miserichords. There are late medieval pews in the north aisle. Parts of 17th century pews with the date 1632 are reused as panelling in the porch upper room.

Interior of Tideswell Church

Tideswell Church

The oldest monuments are two defaced effigies of the late 13th and early 14th century in the north transept. The brass to John Foljambe, sponsor of the chancel, is a copy of 1875. A fine alabaster effigy perhaps of Sir Thurstan de Bower, d1423, co-founder of the Guild of St Mary which used the present Lady Chapel, lies in the south transept. A brass with a figure of God holding Christ Crucified lies on top of a modern tomb chest with a cadaver below of Sampson Meverill, d1462. In the south aisle are brasses of Sir Robert Lytton, d1483, and his wife. In the chancel is a pre-Reformation style brass to Bishop Pursglove, d1579, a noted "Popish" conservative.

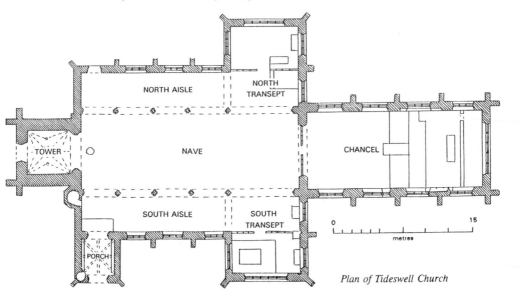

Plan of Tideswell Church

Doorway at Trusley Church

Tissington Church

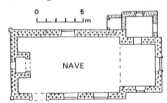

NAVE

Plan of Trusley Church

TISSINGTON   *St Mary*   SK 176523

The Norman west tower has one slender original north window with a roll-moulding and four later heavy buttresses. Also Norman are the font with incised animals and a snake, and the nave and the chancel arch with colonettes and chevrons. The south doorway has an order of colonettes with one volute capital and one with scallops, and a tympanum with figures either side of a chequerboard field. The north aisle was added in 1854 and about the same time the chancel was rebuilt, a porch added, and the south windows replaced. There is a fine communion rail of c1600 and also a two decker pulpit. A wall-monument has two tiers of kneeling figures depicting Francis Fitzherbert, d1619, and his two wives, and his son Sir John, d1643, and his wife. The best of various tablets to members of the Fitzherbert family in the chancel are those of Mary, d1677, and Martha, d1699.

TRUSLEY   *All Saints*   SK 254355

The small brick church of 1713 has a short nave, a lower chancel and a west tower. The windows are arched with stone surrounds. The entrance has a scolly pediment. The box pews, three decker pulpit, communion rails and baluster-shaped font are all of the same period. In the chancel is an incised slab to Bridget Curzon, d1628.

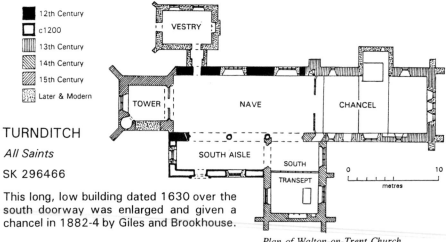

12th Century
c1200
13th Century
14th Century
15th Century
Later & Modern

VESTRY

TOWER | NAVE | CHANCEL

SOUTH AISLE

SOUTH TRANSEPT

0 ___ 10
metres

Plan of Walton-on-Trent Church

TURNDITCH

All Saints

SK 296466

This long, low building dated 1630 over the south doorway was enlarged and given a chancel in 1882-4 by Giles and Brookhouse.

TWYFORD   *St Andrew*   SK 328286

The Norman chancel arch is narrow with chevrons on it. The tower has a 13th century lower stage with a lancet, and a 15th century upper stage with a spire recessed behind battlements. The chancel is 14th century. In the 18th century the nave was remodelled with brick, now delightfully covered with ivy.

UPPER LANGWITH   *Holy Cross*   SK 518694

The chancel has one long lancet on the south side. The nave may also have 13th century masonry but the other windows are mostly 15th century, the period of the south porch with big pinnacles and a vault with transverse arches. The bellcote was added by Norman Shaw at his restoration of 1877.

WALTON-UPON-TRENT   *St Laurence*   SK 216182

The Late Norman south arcade of three bays has circular piers with leaf capitals and two step arches with a slight chamfer on the outer step. At the west end are remains of a window which existed before the arcade did, and the narrow north doorway now leading to an almost detached vestry looks Early Norman. The chancel is 13th century but only the SW lancet was left alone in Street's restoration of 1868. The south transept is of the time of the Waley Chantry founded in it in 1334. It has a squint, sedilia and a piscina and a low recess with a defaced effigy. The diagonally buttressed 15th century tower has a blocked arch of uncertain purpose in its south wall. In the chancel are a brass of Rector Robert Morley, d1492, a half-figure of the divine Thomas Bearcroft, d1680, and three 17th century incised alabaster slabs.

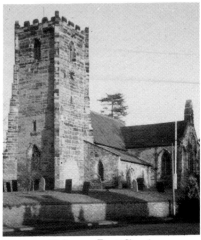

Walton-on-Trent Church

WEST HALLAM   *St Wilfrid*   SK 432411

The north arcade with octagonal piers may be 13th century, and the west tower and several windows are 15th century. The south aisle with its arcade and renewed two-light windows with straight heads is 14th century, as is the chancel, although its east window is renewed. The communion rail is Elizabethan. There is an incised slab of Thomas Powtrell, d1484, and on a tomb chest are recumbent alabaster effigies of Walter Powtrell, d1598, and his wife.

WESTON-UPON-TRENT   *St Mary*   SK 397276

The church lies close to the river and is mostly 13th century, having tall circular piers to the arcades, making the interior seem more spacious than it actually is. The chancel is lower and has lancets with chamfered inner arches and an original doorway. The south aisle has a piscina with a trefoiled head and windows with three stepped lancets and a similar east window but with a circle over the middle lancet. The north aisle windows are 14th century. The west tower has 15th century windows and a recessed spire. The timber framed south porch is 17th century. The font is dated 1661, and the pulpit is dated 1611. The bier and chest are of 1653 and 1662 respectively. There is a fragmentary monument with a skeleton with a pick and shovel and kneeling effigies of Richard Sale, d1615, and his wife.

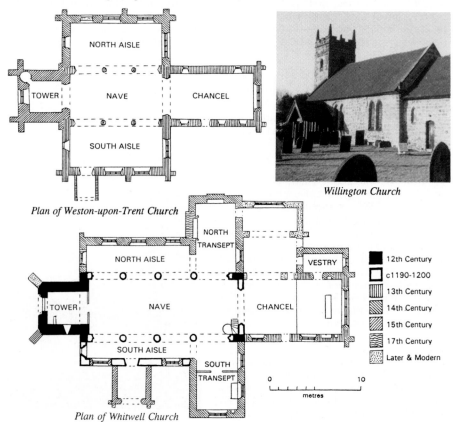

Willington Church

Plan of Weston-upon-Trent Church

Plan of Whitwell Church

WHITWELL   *St Lawrence*   SK 516769

The Norman west tower has a west doorway with one order of colonettes with leaf capitals and chevrons on the arch. The bell openings were blocked when the tower was given a new bell-stage above with battlements and pinnacles in the 15th century. The nave and its clerestory are Norman too, the latter a rarity, and also the chancel, both these parts having corbel tables. The arcades with circular piers and keeled east responds and the chancel arch with waterleaf and scalloped capitals are of the end of the Norman period. In the early 14th century the transepts were added and chancel was remodelled. The transepts have windows with flowing tracery whilst those in the chancel are earlier with quatrefoils and circled trefoils. There are finely decorated sedilia and a niche opposite perhaps intended as a miniature Easter Sepulchre. The font is Norman and there is Jacobean panelling in the chancel. A wall-monument has a recumbent armoured effigy of Sir Roger Manners, d1632.

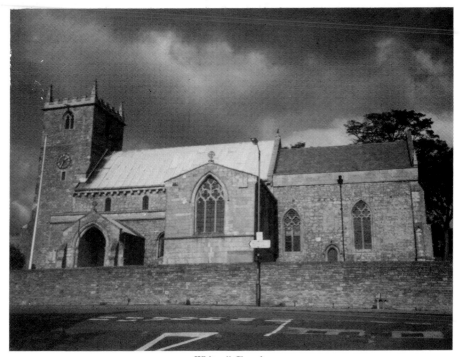

Whitwell Church

WILLINGTON   *St Michael*   SK 295282

In the 16th century the church is recorded as dedicated to St Mary. The south doorway is Norman with a defaced tympanum. Of 1824 are the north transept, the small west tower, the coupled lancets in the south wall, probably the white plaster ceilings and possibly the chancel lancets. The 18th century baluster font is richly acanthus-ornamented.

Wilne Church

WILNE   *St Chad*   SK 448319

The church lies near the Derwent, outside the village. The lower part of the tower with a rectangular stair turret is 13th century, the embattled upper part being later. The south aisle has windows of three lancet lights with the centre one higher than the others, i.e, c1300, and the arcade with octagonal piers is of the same period. The battlements, the low clerestory and the south porch with a pointed tunnel-vault with transverse arches are 15th century additions. The north windows are 14th century. The church was accurately restored by Currey & Thompson after being gutted by fire in 1917 which destroyed the 16th century roofs and 15th century screen, and theirs are the furnishings save the chest with roundels on the front and the font created from part of a Saxon cross shaft carved with dragons and birds. There is a damaged incised alabaster slab to Hugh Willoughby, d1491, and his wife on the nave floor, and there are brasses with kneeling figures of Hugh Willoughby, d1513, and his wife Isabella Clifton. The Willoughby Chapel on the south side was built by Sir Henry in 1622 as a memorial to his father Sir John, d1605, and mother Frances, d1602.

WINGERWORTH   *All Saints*   SK 383675

Norman are the small and low chancel arch with on one side contemporary wall paintings of a Head of Christ and four saints in roundels, the large tub font, the south doorway with one order of colonettes, and the three bay north arcade with round single-chamfered arches on circular piers. There is another round arch of a former aisle or transept in the south outer wall. The chancel has 13th century lancets but has been refaced. In the 15th century the church was given a diagonally buttressed west tower, a clerestory, and battlements throughout. The Hunloke family added a mausoleum on the north side of the chancel in 1783. The church was dramatically re-modelled in 1963-4 by Naylor, Sale & Widdows, when a new nave with pre-cast concrete arches was built at right-angles to the old one, and a semi-circular apse built beyond it. A rare survival is the 15th century rood loft fixed to the wall above the chancel arch instead of being set on a screen (see photo on page 12). It has ribs and bosses underneath, a moulded beam at the front and crenellation at the top. There is an effigy of a 13th century priest with a chalice lying below his folded hands.

WINSTER   *St John the Baptist*   SK 239605

Winster was a chapel-of-ease to Youlgreave until 1838. The font appears to be a Tudor imitation of Norman work. The tower with segmental-headed windows is of 1721. The rest was rebuilt in 1840-2 and remodelled in 1883 to make the church two-aisled with diagonal arches connecting the arcade to chancel arch.

Wirksworth Church

WIRKSWORTH   *St Mary*   SK 287539

This is a large church mostly of c1275-1300 with an aisled nave, a crossing tower with transepts with east aisles, and an aisled chancel. Much of it is restored, the west window being by William Maskrey in 1813, the chancel east window being of 1855, whilst during Sir George Gilbert Scott's restoration of 1870-6 the clerestory was added, the lancets of the chancel and the north transept west wall were renewed and the transept aisles remodelled, these last parts having been widened in 1820 to contain galleries to accommodate the then fast growing congregation. The crossing arches are massive and have some keeling and nailhead decoration. The upper parts of the tower are early 14th century and feature a quatrefoil frieze instead of a parapet, and a lead-covered spike rather than a true spire. The nave is wider than the chancel and has arcades of three bays with quatrefoil-shaped piers with shafts. The south porch is roofed with pitched stone slabs. There are a few unrestored 15th century windows in the north aisle and the transepts.

The Saxon coffin-lid of c1800, discovered in 1820, is an important relic of the sarcophagus of an unknown saint buried here. It has carvings of Christ washing the Disciples' feet, A Crucifixion with the Lamb on a Greek Cross, the Burial of the Virgin, the Presentation in the Temple, the Decent into Hell, the Ascension, the Annunciation, and St Peter receiving a scroll from the Virgin and Child. The transepts contain a number of fragments from a fine Norman church once on this site, from which a font also remains, although there is another font of 1662. In the north transept is a foliated cross with a sword and a forester's horn, and there are brasses of Thomas Blackwell, d1525, and his wife, plus some figures from another Blackwell brass. In the chancel is a fine monument in the then new Renaissance style with an effigy of Anthony Lowe, d1555. In the chancel north aisle is an incised alabaster slab probably made by the Royleys of Burton-on-Trent to Ralph Gell, d1564, and his two wives. In the north chapel is a tomb chest with an effigy of Anthony Gell, d1583.

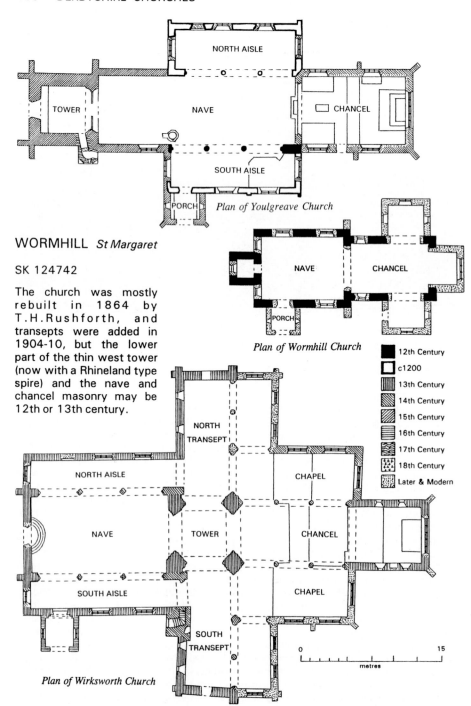

Plan of Youlgreave Church

WORMHILL *St Margaret*

SK 124742

The church was mostly rebuilt in 1864 by T.H.Rushforth, and transepts were added in 1904-10, but the lower part of the thin west tower (now with a Rhineland type spire) and the nave and chancel masonry may be 12th or 13th century.

Plan of Wormhill Church

■	12th Century
□	c1200
	13th Century
	14th Century
	15th Century
	16th Century
	17th Century
	18th Century
	Later & Modern

Plan of Wirksworth Church

Youlgreave Church

YOULGREAVE   *All Saints*   SK 213644

The lofty 15th century west tower has angle buttresses with many set-offs, a SE stair turret only rising half the height of the tower, and pairs of two-light bell-openings, above which are battlements with eight pinnacles. The tower stands somewhat to the west of where the Norman church ended and was connected by an added section of nave without aisles. The nave eastern part has a Late Norman south arcade of three bays with scalloped capitals on circular piers and double chamfered round arches. The north arcade has pointed arcades and a keeled west respond and must be of c1200-10, as opposed to that of c1180 opposite. The south aisle windows have Y-tracery and intersected tracery of c1300. The north aisle and the chancel windows are 15th century, the chancel east window being of five lights. The plain mullioned clerestory windows may be early 16th century, the period of the nave roof and battlements. There was a sensitive restoration in 1869-70 by Norman Shaw.

    The pride of the church is the remarkable font of c1200 carved with animals, and fleur-de-lis, and having the unique feature of a separate projecting side stoup. It was transferred here from Elton in 1838, having been cast out when that church was restored. In the nave north wall is a small arched panel with a figure of a pilgrim in a cloak. By the chancel north wall is an effigy of a cross-legged knight of c1325, thought to be Sir John Rossington. There is a small but fine effigy on a tomb chest of the young Thomas Cockayne, killed in 1488 in a brawl at Polesworth. The fine oblong alabaster panel with a seated Virgin and kneeling figures of Robert Gylbert, d1492, and his wife and children probably formed part of the reredos panel of the Lady Chapel chantry altar at the east end of the south aisle. An inscription refers to Robert providing the chantry with a parclose screen. The brass to Frideswide Gilbert, d1603, was set up by her brother John, a London merchant. A wall monument has kneeling figures of Roger Rowe, d1613, and his wife. In the churchyard is a sundial of 1752 on an upturned font.

OTHER ANGLICAN CHURCHES IN DERBYSHIRE

ALLENTON - St Edmund - 1939 by Eaton of Derby.
ALLESTREE - St Nicholas - 1957-8 by Peter Woore.
AMBERGATE - St Anne - 1890s by A.Coke Hill.
ASHBOURNE - St John Baptist - 1871 by Rundbogenstil for Francis Wright.
ATLOW - St Philip & St James - Rebuilt in 1874 by H.I.Stevens.
BAMFORD - St John the Baptist - 1856-60 by Butterfield.
BARROW HILL - St Andrew - 1893-5 by Parker & Unwin.
BELPER - Christchurch - 1849 by H.I.Stevens.
BELPER - St Peter - 1824 by Habershon.
BIGGIN-BY-HARTINGTON- St Thomas - 1844-8 by E.H.Shellard.
BIRDHOLME - St Augustine - 1931 by Hicks & Charlwood.
BRETBY - St Wystan - Rebuilt 1877.
BRIMINGTON - St Michael - Tower of 1796, nave rebuilt 1847, chancel added 1891.
BURBAGE - Christchurch - 1860 by H.Currey.
BUXTON - St John the Baptist - 1811 by John White, east end remodelled 1896-7.
BUXTON - St Mary the Virgin - 1914-15 by P.Currey and C.C.Thompson
BUXWORTH - St James - 1874 by J.Lowe.
CALOW - St Peter - 1869 by S.Rollinson, tower and spire added 1887.
CHADDESDEN - St Mark - 1938 by Naylor, Sale & Widdows.
CHADDESDEN - St Philip - 1954-6 by Milburn and Partners.
CHAPEL-EN-LE-FRITH - 1903.
CHARLESWORTH - St John the Baptist - 1848-9 by J.Mitchell.
CHINLEY - St Mary - 1907 with east extension of 1957-72 by J.B.Blagney.
CLAY CROSS - St Bartholomew - 1851 by Stevens. Vestry 1858-9 by Street.
CLIFTON - Holy Trinity - 1845 by H.I.Stevens. Apse and tower added 1868.
COTMANHAY - Christ Church - 1847-8 by Stevens.
COTON-IN-THE-ELMS - St Mary - 1844-6 by Stevens.
CRESSWELL - St Mary Magdalene - 1899 by Ambler. Aisles 1914, tower 1927.
CROMFORD - St Mary - 1790s, gothicised and apsidal chancel added in 1858.
CURBAR - All Saints - 1868 by Salvin Junior.
DARLEY ABBEY - St Matthew - 1818-9 by Moses Wood. Chancel added 1885-91.
DERBY - Christchurch - 1834-41 by Habershon. Chancel added 1865.
DERBY - St Andrew - Demolished 1971. Social Security Office on site.
DERBY - St Anne - 1871 by F.W.Hunt in the style of Butterfield.
DERBY - St Augustine - 1897-1908 by Naylor & Sale.
DERBY - St Barnabas - 1880 by A,Coke-Hill. Cruciform 18th century font.
DERBY - St Bartholomew - 1927 by Currey & Thompson. Apse & vestry 1966-9.
DERBY - St Chad - 1881-2 by H.Turner.
DERBY - St Francis - 1953-4 by Milburn & Partners.
DERBY - St James - 1867 by J.Peacock.
DERBY - St Luke - 1872 by F.J.Robinson of Derby.
DERBY - St John the Evangelist - 1826-7 by Francis Goodwin, chancel 1871.
DERBY - St Thomas the Apostle - 1881 by J.Peacock.
DRAYCOTT - St Mary - 1836, originally a Methodist chapel.
EDALE - Holy Trinity - 1885-6 by William Dawes, broach-spire completed 1889.
FAIRFIELD - St Peter - 1839 by local schoolmaster William Swann.
FERNILEE - Holy Trinity - 1904-5 by Currey and Thompson, chancel added 1922-3.
FOOLOW - Small 19th century building next to a chapel of 1836.
GLOSSOP - St James - 1844-6 by E.H.Shellard, chancel enlarged in 1897.
HADFIELD - St Andrew - 1874 by M.& H. Taylor, enlarged in 1923 by C.M.Hadfield.
HASLAND - St Paul - 1850-1 by T.C.Hine.
HAZELWOOD - St John - 1840 by Stevens, restored after a fire in 1902.

HOLLOWAY - Christ Church - 1901-3 by P.H.Currey.
HOLMESFIELD - St Swithin - 1826, chancel added 1897, enlarged 1963.
HORSLEY WOODHOUSE - St Susanna - 1878 by Robinson.
HULLAND - Christ Church - 1838 by John Mason, with contemporary furnishings.
IDRIDGEHAY - St James - 1844-5 by Stevens.
ILKESTON - St Bartholomew - 1895 by Currey. Now used by St John Ambulance.
ILKESTON - St John Evangelist - 1894 by Currey.
LITTLE CHESTER - St Paul - 1849 by Barry & Brown, aisle 1897 by P.H.Currey.
LITTLE EATON - St Paul - 1791, enlarged 1837, remodelled 1851.
LITTLEMOOR - St John Evangelist - 1887, with wide aisles added in 1957.
LITTON - Christ Church - 1926-7 by W.H.R.Blacking. 18th century font brought in.
LONG EATON - St John Evangelist - 1922 by Sir Charles Nicholson.
LOSCOE - St Luke - 1936 by Bernard Widdows.
LOUNDSLEY GREEN - Small, 1960s, overshadowed by Methodist church opposite.
MATLOCK - Holy Trinity - 1842 by Weightman & Hadfield. Enlarged 1873-4.
MIDDLETON-BY-WIRKSWORTH - Holy Trinity - 1844 by Newton.
NEW BRAMPTON - St Thomas - 1830-2 by Woodhead & Hurst. Chancel added 1891.
NEW MILLS - St George - 1829-30 by R.D.Chantrell. Chancel added 1897-8.
NEW MILLS - St James the Less - 1878-80 by W.Swinfen Barber.
OSMASTON - St Martin - 1845 by Stevens.
OSMASTON - St Oswald - 1904 by P.H.Currey.
OVERSEAL - St Matthew - 1840-1 by Thomas Johnson.
PEAK FOREST - King Charles The Martyr - 1660s, entirely rebuilt 1876-7.
RIDDINGS - St James - 1832 by Francis Bedford.
RIDGEWAY - St John - 1838-40 by Woodhead & Hurst, tower 1883-4.
RIPLEY - All Saints - 1820-1, baptistry added 1921.
SHARDLOW - St James - 1838 by Stevens.
SMALLEY - St John the Baptist - Founded 1793, but now of 1844, 1862 and 1912.
SOMERCOTES - St Thomas - East parts 1854, rest of 1902 by P.H.Currey.
STONEGRAVELS- Christ Church - 1869 by S. Rollinson, aisles added 1913-14.
SWADLINCOTE - Emanuel - 1848 by Stevens.
SWANWICK -St Andrew - 1859-60 by Benjamin Wilson, SW tower added 1902.
TANSLEY - Holy Trinity - 1839-40 by John Mason. North aisle added 1869.
WENSLEY - St Mary - 1841-3 by Weightman & Hadfield, chancel added 1866.
WHITTINGTON - St Bartholomew - 1896 by E.R.Rollinson, but with older plate.
WOODVILLE - St Stephen - 1846.
YEAVELEY - Holy Trinity - 1840.

FURTHER READING

Alabaster Tombs, A.Gardner, 1940.
Derbyshire, Roy Christian, 1978.
Derbyshire, Little Guides series,
    J.C.Cox, 1903.
Derbyshire, Buildings of England series,
    Nikolaus Pevsner, 1953.
Fonts, E.Tyrell Green, 1928.
Notes on the Churches of Derbyshire,
    J.C.Cox, 4 Volumes, 1875-9.

Cockayne Tomb at Youlgreave

GLOSSARY OF ARCHITECTURAL TERMS

Apse	- Semi-circular or polygonal east end of a church containing an altar.
Ashlar	- Masonry of blocks with even faces and square edges.
Baroque	- A whimsical and odd form of the Classical architectural style.
Beakhead	- Decorative motif of bird or beast heads, often biting a roll moulding.
Broaches	- Sloping half pyramids adapting an octagonal spire to a square tower.
Cartouche	- A tablet with ornate frame, usually enclosing an inscription.
Caryatid	- Female figure supporting an architectural member.
Chancel	- The eastern part of a church used by the clergy.
Chevron Ornament	- A Norman ornament with continuous Vs forming a zig-zag.
Clerestory	- An upper storey pierced by windows lighting the floor below.
Collar Beam	- A tie-beam used higher up near the apex of the roof.
Crossing Tower	- A tower built on four arches in the middle of a cruciform church.
Cruciform Church	- A cross-shaped church with transepts forming the arms of the cross.
Cusp	- A projecting point between the foils of a foiled Gothic arch.
Dado	- The decorative covering of the lower part of a wall or screen.
Decorated	- The architecture style in vogue in England c1300-1380.
Dog Tooth	- Four centered stars placed diagonally and raised pyramidally.
Easter Sepulchre	- A recess in a chancel which received an effigy of Christ at Easter.
Elizabethan	- Of the time of Queen Elizabeth I (1558-1603).
Fan Vault	- Vault with fan-like patterns. In fashion from c1440 to 1530.
Foil	- A lobe formed by the cusping of a circle or arch.
Four Centred Arch	- A low, flattish arch with each curve drawn from two compass points.
Head Stops	- Heads of humans or beasts forming the ends of a hoodmould.
Hoodmould	- A projecting moulding above a lintel or arch to throw off water.
Impost	- A wall bracket, often moulded, to support the end of an arch.
Jacobean	- Of the time of King James I (1603-25).
Jamb	- The side of a doorway, window, or other opening.
Lancet	- A long and comparatively narrow window with a pointed head.
Light	- A compartment of a window.
Lintel	- A horizontal stone or beam spanning an opening.
Miserichord	- Bracket underneath hinged choir stall seat to support standing person.
Mullion	- A vertical member dividing the lights of a window.
Nave	- The part of a church in which the congregation sits or stands.
Nook-Shaft	- A shaft set in the angle of a pier or respond or jamb of a window.
Norman	- A division of English Romanesque architecture from 1066 to 1200.
Ogival Arch	- Arch of oriental origin with both convex and concave curves.
Pediment	- Low-pitch gable used in classical and neo-classical architecture.
Perpendicular	- The architectural style in vogue in England c1380-1540.
Pilaster	- Flat buttress or pier attached to a wall.
Piscina	- A stone basin used for rinsing out holy vessels after a mass.
Quoins	- Dressed stones at the corners of a building.
Reredos	- Structure behind and above an altar forming a backdrop to it.
Respond	- A half pier or column bonded into a wall and carrying an arch.
Reticulation	- Tracery with a net-like appearence. Current c1330-70.
Rococo	- The late phase of the Baroque style, current in mid 18th century.
Rood Screen	- A screen with a crucifix mounted on it between a nave and chancel.
Sedilia	- Seats for clergy (usually three) in the south wall of a chancel.
Spandrel	- The surface between two arches.
Tester	- A sounding board above a 17th or 18th century pulpit.
Tie-Beam	- A beam connecting the slopes of a roof at or near its foot.
Tracery	- Intersecting ribwork in the upper part of a later Gothic window.
Transom	- A horizontal member dividing the lights of a window.
Tuscan	- An order of Classical architecture.
Tympanum	- The space between the lintel of a doorway and the arch above it.
Venetian Window	- Window with a square headed light on either side of an arched light.
Voussoir	- Wedge-shaped stone forming part of an arch.